The Narc Decoder

Understanding the Language of the Narcissist

By Tina Marie Swithin

Dedicated to the warriors who have buckled to their knees as a result of the harsh words dealt by someone with a Cluster B Personality Disorder such as Narcissistic Personality Disorder, Borderline Personality Disorder or Antisocial Personality Disorder. Unless you have traveled this very rocky, treacherous road, it is difficult to understand the trials, tribulations and heartbreak.

Cheers to the light at the end of a long, dark tunnel.

It is there, I promise.

FINE PRINT

In *The Narc Decoder*, author, Tina Swithin is offering her own personal perspectives on the subject matter of personal healing and growth during a high-conflict divorce. This book is not intended to offer legal, psychological or therapeutic advice nor should it be used for that purpose.

The author is not responsible for personal decisions based on the subject matter contained in this book. You are advised to seek professional assistance in your area of residence with individuals who are qualified to help you with legal advice or guidance.

Please Note: Narcissistic Personality Disorder (NPD) affects both males and females. Throughout this book, the author is referencing her experience with her ex-husband, but she is no way implying that this issue is isolated to one gender. Tina provides support, advocacy and guidance to both males and females on her blog and through her consulting business. Tina is pro-child and does not align with mother's rights groups or father's rights groups.

Contact Information:
Tina Swithin
PO Box 123, San Luis Obispo, California 93406
tina@tinaswithin.com
www.tinaswithin.com or www.thelemonadeclub.com

Cover Design: Leukothea Design

Editing: Ginna French DuRard, Rebecca Binny and Kari Herreman

ISBN-13: 978-0692644485
ISBN-10: 0692644482

TABLE OF CONTENTS

FOREWORD

By J. Paul Shirley

Tina Swithin's new book, The Narc Decoder, is a masterful blend of penetrating insight and sound practical advice. Tina generously shares her own life journey as a vehicle for her own hard-won knowledge about narcissism - a precious gift, in my opinion - for nothing more than the price of a book. Tina has a unique way of inviting the reader to sit down at her kitchen table and enjoy a warm cup of tea together. Don't let the comfort level fool you, though, because it is only the beginning. Any truly realistic discussion of narcissism must of necessity be factually down-and-dirty, and Tina does not shy away from the task.

Tina clearly understands the technical aspects of the topic, i.e., the underlying psychological dynamics of Cluster B personality disorders. Equally important (if not more so), she understands the toxic concrete ways in which those disorders manifest in interpersonal relationships. Her knowledge alone, however, is not where the power of this book comes from. The power of Tina's writing can be summarized in two words: "simple" and "accurate."

Tina's work is easy to read, flowing easily from page to page, and from chapter to chapter, but interspersed with the easy flow is embedded the absolutely essential brutally hard, clinically cold information, which is a necessary component to changing from being a yielding victim to narcissistic behavior. At the risk of sounding too cutely poetic, Tina's writing about narcissism reminds me of old descriptions of the world-famous great boxing master, Mohammed Ali, whose incredible smoothness in the ring was combined with punches that were hard and deadly accurate.

In this book, Tina really does float like a butterfly and sting like a bee. In contrast, the cold clinical descriptions found in the diagnostic manual pale by comparison, and are (unfortunately) of limited help in guiding a real flesh-and-blood person to find her way through the quagmire and on to the empowering knowledge, strength, and behavior that will empower her to stand up to the raw brutality of narcissism.

Tina lets the reader know that she's been there. Although she offers the cold-scalpel truth of how the brutal B-Cluster behaviors can be in taking a relationship and "nuking" it to oblivion, she also intersperses kind words of reassurance that say to the reader, "It's all right. I've been there. It is choppy water, but it is possible to get through and across to the other side. I know because I've done it, and together, hand in hand with me, you can do it too." This unusual blend of calm reassurance, cold clinical facts and warm encouragement is rare, and most often is to be found only in a good relationship with a skilled therapist. Tina manages to convey all of that essence in her book. Her skill, combined with knowledge and warmth, tell me that Tina has a true gift of being able to speak to many levels - the heart, the head, and the soul - all at once. Even despite the years I spent working in a maximum security state prison, some of Tina's descriptions of narcissism's brutality chilled me. At the same time, her calm reassurance offered feelings of encouragement.

There is a growing body of good work on narcissism, and in my opinion, Tina's ranks up there with the very best of them. I have had the unique opportunity of working closely with a gifted writer in the past, and I have come to deeply appreciate good writing that comes from the heart, soul, and mind all at the same time. If you have a need to deal with narcissism, I highly recommend that you get Tina's book and read it. It is short and easy to read, but it packs a wallop. I predict you will come away from it changed - for the better.

As I started reading this book, I was poised to welcome Tina Swithin as a new colleague into the ranks of writers about Cluster B personality disorders. However, in reading her book, I have found myself instead becoming her fan. Thank you, Tina, for this inspiring and ground-breaking new book on a difficult topic that continues to have a crying need for helpful information." **-J. Paul Shirley, MSW and Co-Author of "Stop Walking on Eggshells" Workbook**

CHAPTER 1

UNDERSTANDING NARC-ISH

In my mid-twenties, I contemplated learning multiple foreign languages. I envisioned dabbling in French to successfully make my way around Paris or Irish Gaelic to explore the rich history of Ireland along with my deep ancestral roots in that country. My day dreams about learning new languages always went hand in hand with the imagery of world travel. The thought of exploring exotic and old world places far away from home intrigued me. My mind summoned several foreign adventures, but never did I think I would need to learn a foreign language to navigate my own life.

In 2008, I heard the words, "Narcissistic Personality Disorder" (NPD) to describe my then-husband, Seth. It took a couple years for the reality of those three little words to really sink in. Looking back, the red flags had been waving in the wind since our very first date. Those flags grew taller and more vibrant in color during our marriage. As it turns out, those same red flags that had been lining my path for years were dipped in a highly flammable mixture of kerosene. I realized the danger only when they exploded near the end of my marriage. Like any unexpected explosion, I was unprepared and left nursing deep, emotional, third-degree burns.

During our marriage, Seth recalled a childhood that would leave most green with envy. He was the most popular student in his Catholic school and the captain of every sports team. He was a surfer who had grown up on the beach and all of the girls adored him. If we ran into someone around town who resembled Barbie or a famous super model, he had surely dated her somewhere between preschool and college. Seth's older brother, Robert (with whom he had a bizarre, competitive relationship) was the first to mention that Seth's version of his childhood differed greatly from reality. "Seth's stories of his childhood leave my family baffled," said Robert. He went on to explain, "My parents and I are often left wondering where we were during all of these grand adventures and surfing expeditions that he boasts about. I grew up surfing but Seth stayed in the shallow waves on a boogie board." During our marriage, Seth kept multiple surf boards in our garage and his license plate frame was from the Surf Rider Foundation. The reality was, Seth was intimidated by the ocean and envious of his brother and cousins who did spend their days riding waves.

Shortly after the encounter with Seth's brother, a mutual friend who grew up with Seth told a story which portrayed Seth as shy, studious, unpopular and socially awkward. Instead of identifying this revelation as a red flag, I felt sorry for Seth. In my empathic mind, it was sad that Seth was trying to impress me with these stories because in reality, he was embarrassed about his imperfect, lonely childhood. His parents both worked in education and spent long hours at the school leaving Seth with nannies or walking the empty school campuses alone. They did a wonderful job touting themselves as the picture-perfect family, but the reality behind the scenes was not as pretty. Seth's father is as narcissistic as they come and has spent much of the marriage bedding other women and using the silent treatment for weeks on end to punish his wife if she makes so much as a peep about his adulterous ways.

After hearing the 94th story about Seth surfing the waves in Avila Beach, California as an elementary school child, I confronted him one evening while we were on vacation in Las Vegas. My goal was to let him know that I knew the truth and that I still loved him. I couldn't listen to another story knowing they were all lies. I was physically uncomfortable each time he started to spin a new tale to impress me. "Seth – I ran into Sandy Rodrigues and I know the truth about your childhood. It's okay…I understand." Initially Seth was defensive and became very quiet. He physically pulled away from me and looked pained. In that moment, Seth resembled a broken six-year old boy. He appeared wounded, but didn't deny the facts.

Seth's solution was to drink copious amounts of alcohol and sulkily retreat into a punitive silence. The silent treatment would last for weeks and was the first of many times when Seth would refuse to speak to me. How dare I apply the truth and vanquish his fictional storyline which seemed so believable. In essence, he was training me early on to keep my mouth closed. I learned quickly that bringing half-truths or lies to the surface would result in being emotionally shut out by my husband. He withdrew physically, emotionally and verbally. While he was initially caught off guard, his eyes grew cold, dark and distant as the night progressed and there was an underlying look of rage that frightened me and sent shivers down my spine. My *Prince Charming* had been replaced by someone whom I no longer recognized. The most terrifying part for me (and the one that I couldn't seem to get out of my head) was how believable his stories were prior to the rug being pulled out from under him.

The lies continued throughout our seven-year marriage and the silent treatments increased in severity and longevity. Seth used work, alcohol and triathlons to escape from anything that he perceived as criticism or conflict. I learned to bottle things up because things were less hostile this way. Everything was my fault during the difficult times, but anytime there was a business success or an opportunity for press in our companies, Seth took full responsibility and left me in the shadows. His drive to impress those in our inner and outer circle of friends seemed to go into overdrive once I began to see a clear picture of who Seth really was. My designated role was to continue the façade of the "happy family" to the outside world and if I didn't, I was the enemy and there was a price to pay. I was being forced into the same role that his mother had carried for over 30 years of marriage. Living a pretend, fake life was eating at me night and day.

Toward the end of our marriage and after begging and pleading with Seth, we started marriage counseling. After a few months, our therapist refused to meet with Seth alone. This heightened my concerns about Seth and his credibility. Originally, he had planned to meet with both of us individually and then together as a couple. The therapist explained that he needed me present to deliver accurate information in the counseling sessions. When Seth attended individual sessions, he would spin stories and justify his deceitful actions which seemed to be at the forefront of our need for therapy.

During our joint therapy sessions, I was able to calmly point out the truth and then Seth would backtrack. It was like a predictable dance that took place every week. The therapist would corner Seth on his lies and lack of remorse, which would cause Seth to talk in circles. Seth was highly skilled at squirming his way out of these situations. I'm sure this dance was as fascinating for the therapist to observe from a clinical standpoint as it was tragic for me to realize this was my life and marriage. He really seemed to believe what he was saying even when confronted with harsh reality. His commitment to his version of reality led him to create a labyrinth of lies. When he began talking in circles, he would create a new truth. By the time he was done, I was left so confused and baffled that I didn't even remember where the truth ended and the lies began! After six months of therapy, it was clear that our marriage was damaged to the point of no return. I wrongfully assumed that Seth would take the same stance of avoiding conflict that he had taken during our marriage, but that was not the case.

The first six-months of our separation were fairly uneventful to the point that we even took the girls on a family trip to Disneyland for their birthdays. I had been emotionally checked out from the relationship for so long and naively believed that it would be possible to have a friendship with Seth once the dust settled. Seth seemed perfectly content in his new life four hours north of us and quickly began to date through online dating sites. Oddly, I wasn't fazed by the thought of him dating. I saw it as a catalyst for him to move forward in his life while giving me room to breathe, rebuild myself and begin my new life as a single mom. When I began dating my now-husband, Glenn, six-months post separation, the real nightmare of divorcing a narcissist began to haunt my days and nights. Seth never envisioned that I would begin dating and in all honesty, it was never my intention. It turns out that there was a double standard in play and suddenly, Seth wanted me back. When I denied his pleas to make our marriage work, all hell broke loose.

To a narcissist, things are black or white. There is no grey area. Seth had declared all-out war and I was the marked enemy. Seth's lies were disheartening during my marriage, but they were absolutely petrifying when the stakes were high and his deceptions began spilling into the courtroom. I felt like I was in a fog for the first two years of my divorce and custody proceedings. I was buried deep in court documents and embattled with protecting my daughters, acting as my own attorney and fielding irrational accusations left and right. While the accusations may have been absurd, I was forced to address them and defend myself in court. Although the absurdity ranged from proving that I was not actually running a prostitution ring or guzzling gallon-size bottles of tequila on Monday mornings, I could not take the risk of their acceptance by the court due to my failure to prove them false. I didn't have a revolving door of men filtering in and out of my apartment, nor was I hiding large sums of money in Swiss bank accounts. I had no idea where these allegations were coming from and I found myself confused at every turn. I remember questioning whether or not he was completely delusional and wondered if he really believed the things he was saying. I was baffled on a daily basis and questioned my own sanity more than a time or two.

The more I learned about Narcissistic Personality Disorder (NPD), the more I began to understand my ex-husband's communication style. I learned about projection and deflection, two commonly found tools in any narcissist's toolbox. I also came to realize that unlike the liars I had known in the past, the narcissist will lie even when there is no reason to lie. In addition, they are so convincing that they can often pass lie detector tests. It is difficult to understand if the narcissist actually believes their own fabrications, as they are so convincing. I believe there are a combination of factors at play. My personal theory is that deep down, the narcissist knows they are lying, however their ego and inflated sense of self-worth causes them to believe that everyone should accept the words that leave their mouth as pure truth.

This inflated sense of self-worth is often paired with an unhealthy need for control. The narcissist lives his or her life in a way which forces them to stay in reaction mode. The lies they tell allow them to have some semblance of control. While their own behaviors, habits, emotions, finances, relationships and professional interests are in predictable patterns of chaos, controlling a target satiates the need to feel control. They become masters at controlling someone else's reality, while their own lives fall apart. In short, the narcissist is a convincing liar. While I accepted Seth's delusions during my marriage, the untruths he told to support his distorted reality during my custody battle in a courtroom were threatening to damage my reputation with the Judge who would be presiding over my case.

At the infancy of my divorce, a single email, text or voicemail from Seth could literally knock me to my knees and cause a flood of tears to start flowing. In the beginning, his voicemails were drunk, angry, Charlie Sheen-style rants. With time, and under the advice of his family members and attorneys, he pulled himself together and became much more calculated in his approach. When confronted by the court about one particular series of voicemails in 2009 in which he called me names like, "loser," "white trash," and "slut," he explained to the Commissioner that he was angry due to my promiscuous behavior and infidelity. Apparently, I had slept with four different men in four months. None of this was true, but he seemed to believe it. To my dismay, the Commissioner seemed to take Seth's excuse under consideration as an explanation for his behavior and threats.

Narcissist's love to shift the blame for their own mal-adaptive behavior onto their targets. Seth's favorite phrases involved threats of karma and on one late night tirade, he ended the voicemail by saying, "There is karma in this world and you will just have to deal with it. How do you sleep at night?" The answer to his question: not very well, but thanks for asking! He knew how to threaten me without crossing legal lines and the stalking and harassment was breaking me. I was living in a constant state of terror and hypervigilance. I knew in my heart of hearts that this man was absolutely capable of ending my life and getting away with it. Try telling that to the court or to an attorney and they will quickly label YOU as the lunatic.

I checked my locks multiple times before going to sleep each night and I bolted upright at even the slightest noises. My bedtime companions were a hammer and an industrial sized can of Mace. Seth loved to text me at 1am, 2am and 3am to remind me about karma or to tell me what a horrible mother I was. He was also known to lurk around my apartment so those text messages were chilling reminders that I would never escape him. On one occasion, he left our wedding videos in front of my walkway, but adamantly denied doing it. To someone who hasn't divorced a narcissist, I would appear to be hyper-vigilant, psychotic and paranoid. Someone who has lived this nightmare and walked in my shoes knows, it is an absolutely terrifying reality that becomes daily life.

Over time, living this way can wear a person down until *they* are seen by the courts as the unstable party. The time lost and damage done in battle can cause massive destruction to a person's life. Sadly, I have seen this happen to several of my clients. Although it can be turned around over time with education and determination, it's best not to go down the rabbit hole in the first place. There have been many nights that I lay sobbing with my head on the computer keyboard trying to make sense of Seth's crazy-making emails. There have also been countless hours spent responding to his tirades with paragraphs and paragraphs of wasted time, energy and emotion. My Post Traumatic Stress Disorder (PTSD) went into overdrive every time I was notified about a new message waiting for me. Looking back, it pains me greatly to relive the desperation I felt while trying to explain that I wasn't a drunken, white trash floozy.

Even more than the hurtful, untruthful words, it pains me *more* to reflect on the disgusting "high" Seth received during these times from my reactions. Seth was seeking the intoxicating rush he got knowing that he was successful in engaging me in his twisted, demented scheme to break me down and leave me depleted on every level. Seth's emails kept me operating in a constant state of terror mixed with equal doses of confusion. Through this experience, I discovered that even mental health professionals were baffled by the abusive communication from the narcissist. While they sympathized with the pain I was experiencing, they couldn't really provide insight or any real assistance with handling the communication – nor could they guide me on how to make it stop. Some even seemed to question whether I was exaggerating until I showed them examples of his emails and text messages. As if it wasn't exhausting enough to deal with Seth, I was using any leftover energy to educate those who claimed to be educated in personality disorders.

Just when I thought I was at my breaking point, I began to bury myself in research about NPD. I had heard those three words from a highly respected therapist in my community and the pieces were coming together. Prior to this, I had felt blindsided by Seth's attacks and the overall direction of our custody battle. The more I read, the more I came to understand that the war declared on my head had everything to do with Seth's deep-seeded need to win and control. When our marriage first ended, he had everything he wanted: a new six-figure job, which afforded him the freedom to date and the ability to lavishly spend money without me holding him accountable. On the weekends he came home and played super dad, parading the girls around town in pigtails and perfectly pressed dresses. He expected me to be deep in the throes of depression over our failed marriage while he lived a playboy lifestyle. When he saw that I was happy and moving on in my life, he decided that he wanted to make our marriage work. He was losing control and he went into overdrive.

The more I read, the more I understood the grim reality that I was facing. Much of Seth's behavior was even becoming eerily predictable. If he returned home and I was dressed up, I could predict a slew of attacking emails within hours. He would attack my looks, my intelligence, my past and my future. When a narcissist loses control over his or her victim, they begin a campaign to control how others think of you. My reputation was on the line inside and outside of the courtroom with friends, family members and those in the local business community. At one point, his email attacks were so bad that my Aunt insisted on scanning them to determine if I should read them or not. Her offer to act as my buffer was a welcome reprieve from the escalating abuse.

In my research, I discovered a new language which took quite a bit of studying and insight on NPD to understand. As it turns out, the reason that I was so bewildered by Seth's communication style was that we were speaking completely different languages. I spoke the English version of "human" while he was speaking the non-human "Narc-ish." I am convinced there is a Narc-ish dictionary or manual hidden deep in a dark, musty hole somewhere in a faraway land with step-by-step instructions on how to inflict fear, confusion and despair. From this land, narcissists hail. Their secret language can only be decoded by those who aren't fooled by the narcissist's stealth ability to inflict confusion and chaos with it.

My computer has a feature that allows me to translate most languages. However, this particular area of my life requires technology that is a bit savvier. Need is the catalyst of industry: and I was in need of a device to decipher Narc-ish. So, I invented one. I call it the "Narc Decoder" and have made life-altering good use of it. The good news is, everyone has access to the Narc Decoder because it is a machine that I am honored to replicate and share with anyone who is forced to communicate with a narcissist. Once you understand how to use the Narc Decoder, your life will change for the better. You will become empowered and will regain your voice. Over time, you will begin to find humor in the communication style that once left you on your knees begging for mercy.

When I first invented this fascinating device, I received a lot of hate mail and negative comments. Many thought I was trying to insert humor into a dark subject matter that destroyed lives and affected children. I disagree. Just like humor has been found to help chronically ill patients in hospitals, you *must* find humor whenever possible to make it through this battle. I want to clarify, there is *nothing* humorous about a child or an adult being abused. Period. But, there is humor when it comes to the narcissist. This could be the narcissist's attempt to paint you in a negative light over mismatched socks on your two-year old or the allegation that you arrived .0001 seconds late for a parenting exchange. Some of it is so far reaching that it is funny in a pathetic sort of way. In the worst of human conditions, laughter has preserved humanity. It is essential to making it through this kind of hell without it breaking you.

Over the past five years, I have become fluent in translating and understanding Narc-ish. Prior to 2009, I had never been at the receiving end of such anger, hatred and bizarre accusations. I was often paralyzed by fear, confusion and sadness and riddled with PTSD. The emails and text messages were inundating my phone, my computer and my brain every single day and night. These horrific messages were originating from a person whom I once trusted with my heart, future and finances. The Narc Decoder was my way of reclaiming my power. As I began to educate myself on NPD and this new, foreign language, light bulbs began going off for me. Education and knowledge *is* power. Slowly but surely I began to regain my self-worth. I pulled up my bootstraps and dusted myself off.

As the fog from the narcissistic abuse began to lift, I realized that almost everything Seth accused me of was what he was actually guilty of doing. This is known as *projection*. In the beginning, Seth accused me of being a drunken whore. While I knew my truth, the court did not. The truth was, Seth was a drunkard stumbling through his days. By night, he was desperately *trying* to be a whore. Due to his odd, socially awkward ways, I believe his attempts were mostly futile. Thankfully, Seth was unsuccessful in convincing the courts of my drunken, promiscuous behavior, but he was successful in muddying the waters, which can be equally damaging during a high-conflict custody battle. The Judge sits watching the back-and-forth like a ping-pong ball and becomes frustrated with both sides equally. Fair? No. Harsh reality of a crumbling Family Court System? Yes.

Divorce itself is generally chock full of conflict, but a divorce from a narcissist will elevate the conflict to levels that few people can comprehend. Cluster B individuals are unable to compromise and are fueled like a wildfire by the need to control and win. The vast majority of divorce professionals such as judges, Guardian Ad Litems (GAL), custody evaluators and even psychologists do not truly understand NPD unless they've personally experienced the wrath of a narcissist. Over the years I have spoken to numerous mental health professionals, some being my coaching clients. All of these professionals echo the same sentiments, "You can't learn this in college, in lectures or in books. You can't teach this. You have to live this to truly understand the intricate dynamics of a Cluster B personality disorder and how this disorder affects these individuals as parents. More importantly, how this personality disorder affects the innocent children within their clutches."

CHAPTER 2

PROFILING THE NARCISSIST

In my advocacy work with those who are involved in high-conflict custody battles, I have read thousands and thousands of emails over the years. While many are eerily similar in content, they are also very different based on the intricacies of the individual narcissist. I often ask my coaching clients for the profession of their ex-husband or ex-wife because this provides incredible insight into the inner workings of their minds. It is critical to "profile" your ex-Narcissist almost like the FBI would profile a criminal. If they are in the sales industry, it means they are incredibly skilled at "impression management" because they have been trained to speak smoothly, say all of the right things and throw out a hook to make the sale. If they are in law enforcement or a military position, there are generally more control issues that come with these professions. Knowing thine enemy is critical in any battle; a custody battle is no exception.

While I am talking to clients or those I meet doing my volunteer work, I am often seen scribbling notes in a desperate attempt to understand the inner workings of the narcissist in question. Are they exhibitionists who crave attention and the spotlight, or are they the covert, introverted type who often fly under the radar, but are incredibly calculating in their approach? Are they the elitist, cut-throat, opportunist-type constantly hunting for their next kill in an effort to elevate themselves financially or in status? Do they fall into the amorous, Casanova category, ready to seduce the pants or skirt right off their next conquest? Or do they exhibit several categories? Many individuals with personality disorders also suffer from addiction problems such as drugs, alcohol or pornography.

The narcissists who have exhibitionist qualities will typically cancel their parenting time for social events providing you with documentation that their words in court are not in alignment with their actions. The Narcissists with introverted qualities are generally smarter about what they put in writing. On the other hand, I have seen some who are so disconnected from reality that they provide mountains of documentation for court due to their bizarre, rambling diatribes. The cut-throat opportunist is typically so preoccupied with business and lifestyle choices that they will be distracted by the mundane task of caring for a child until an opportunity arises to showcase the child for attention. The romantic, seductive type is easily distracted by the next blonde that walks by but many times, will use the child to paint an idyllic picture if the new woman craves children and a white-picket fence lifestyle. When addiction issues are in play, the narcissist is not operating at their full potential and this situation often provides opportunity for court documentation.

I place a tremendous amount of weight on the importance of understanding the narcissist in your life. One of my clients, Veronica, is a successful business-woman. Her ex-narcissist, Andy, is a blue collar worker who did not receive a formal education. To clarify, I come from a hard-working, blue collar family, and I do not intend to convey that I am snubbing my nose at this line of work. I am simply using this situation as an example of why it is important to profile and understand the dynamics of the person you are up against. While I was on a call with Veronica, she mentioned that he ex-husband hates when she uses big words during their email exchanges. I suggested she grab a dictionary and begin using the biggest words she can find in every email. To some, this may seem like a manipulative approach, but I disagree. You are dealing with a highly skilled, cunning person and it is your job to push the necessary buttons in an attempt to allow their true colors to show. You are facing a person who thrives on manipulation and you are simply helping to remove the mask of deception in an attempt to protect your children. In Veronica's case, using sophisticated words ensured that her ex-husband would show his true colors in the form of uncontrollable rage which had landed him in hot water throughout his life.

As many of my clients know, I am not one to sugar coat things. I am one of the most positive, optimistic people you will ever meet, but I am also incredibly realistic. It is imperative to remember that when the narcissist is being nice, it's because they have something to gain. Tattoo this on the inside of your left arm or backwards on your forehead if you must, but always remember this as fact. You might as well bang your head into a brick wall if you expect the narcissist to be reasonable, empathetic or human in any way. If you sense or witness any of these traits, there is an ulterior motive. The narcissist would love nothing more than to know you are eating uncooked Top Ramen out of a dumpster for dinner tonight while wearing yesterday's underwear.

A few weeks before Valentine's Day 2010, Seth contacted me and offered to trade weekends so Glenn (boyfriend at the time, now husband) and I could go away on Valentine's Day. I was confused, but at the same time I was starting to catch onto his games. The reality was that Seth hated Glenn. Glenn is nine years older than I am and Seth's favorite pastime is making jabs about Glenn's age. Seth has attempted to push every button that he could find. In a healthy co-parenting relationship, Seth's offer to allow me a Valentine's Day weekend away would have been a thoughtful and generous offer. I responded in a way Seth didn't expect, "No thank you- I will be following the court order as it is written."

Seth exploded. The reality was, Seth wanted to give up his weekend which was just before Valentine's Day so that he could go snowboarding in Utah. I stuck to the schedule and he ended up canceling his parenting time altogether. Prior to this epiphany, I had fallen for Seth's manipulations many times. If I had agreed to go along with Seth's proposed switch, the odds were incredibly high that he would have cancelled Valentine's weekend anyway after I had already made plans, leaving me disappointed and in a childcare bind. He would have been laughing all the way to his expensive dinner at the Montage fresh off the snowy slopes of Utah.

Another reality check while we are on the topic: projection works both ways. While the narcissist is known to project their dark, seedy personas, behaviors and qualities on us, we are known to project our honest, empathetic qualities on them. In other words, because we are truthful, authentic and kind, we expect that the Narcissist has those underlying traits. Big newsflash! They don't! None. Nada. Zilch. Just because I am an honest, sensible person does not mean that everyone else is. This is one of the ways we get ourselves caught in the web of the narcissist in the first place. Always listen to your instinct because your inner voice will never lead you astray. Do not, under any circumstances, project your positive qualities on the narcissist because doing so will set you up for failure and heartache.

CHAPTER 3

COMMUNICATING

WITH A NARCISSIST

Now that you are learning to speak Narc-ish and you are beginning to profile the narcissist in your life, you will need to know how to take what you are learning and put it to use. I recommend that all non-emergency communication should be in writing whenever possible, because we all know the narcissist is highly skilled at twisting words or recreating reality. Anyone who has communicated with a narcissist knows that logic is defied at every turn. If your map says, "turn right," mysteriously the street only goes left. The street goes uphill both ways and the driving conditions are horrendous.

Here are a handful of basic rules that I used to guide me during the five years that I was forced to communicate with Seth:

Rule #1: No Engagement

The number one rule when dealing with a narcissist is simple but critical: no engagement. Similar to a drug addict, narcissists have a deep need to derive emotion from their victims. If a drug dealer stopped selling drugs, the addict would find a new supplier. Stop giving them what they want, which is your time, energy and emotions. Eventually, they will find a new dealer. This is easier said than done if your hands are tied by the Family Court system and you are forced to co-parent or parallel parent. While co-parenting, for lack of a better term, requires communication, it should be limited, business-like and entirely free of emotions. If an email causes you to go into a tailspin, walk away and take a deep breath and have a 24-hour rule before responding to all non-emergency communication.

Rule #2: Decode

When you first unwrap your shiny new Narc Decoder, remember that with any new appliance, it can take time to learn how to use all the bells and whistles. It may take time to process emails in the beginning but with time, it will be effortless. The Narc Decoder can analyze and decipher the most cryptic and bizarre narcissistic emails. An example of a typical narcissistic email would be, "You really need to watch your drinking – I am concerned that you are spiraling out of control. This is a horrible example to be setting in front of the children." A message like this can be placed in the Narc Decoder and translated (Snap, fizzle, pop!) to say, "I have a horrible alcohol problem and I'm completely out of control. You and I both know that I don't care about the example I'm setting for the children because I am completely incapable of caring for anyone – including my own children. My goal is to throw this accusation at you so that the water is muddy and the judge doesn't know who to believe. You're lucky I didn't accuse you of being a drug addict – I'm saving that one for Friday's email."

The Narc Decoder may smoke and rumble, but it will successfully scrub down the projection, lies, attacks and ulterior motives that are typically found in a narcissist's email. When you are learning to use your Narc Decoder, I encourage you to share your decoded messages with your mom, your sister or a best friend. Feeling supported and finding humor in the situation is very liberating, validating and healing. If decoding is too difficult for you in the beginning stages due to PTSD, loan the decoder to a trusted friend or family member and let them decode the message for you. The key is to find humor which will act as a guiding light as you climb out of the darkness.

Rule #3: Gray Rock with Canned Responses and Courtesy

My personal approach is a mixture of the Gray Rock technique, canned responses and good 'ol fashion, "kill 'em with kindness." Many will cringe at the mere thought of showing courtesy to a narcissist, but I ask you to stay with me for a few moments. Using my book for kindling in your fireplace is one option, but I ask you to finish this chapter before you make the decision to grab the matches. I am not suggesting that you go overboard or invite the narcissist out for a cup of coffee. I am suggesting, if you are in a custody battle with a personality disordered individual, that you paint yourself in the most positive light for court as well as your children. Also, I don't mean that your emails have to be filled with sugar and a cherry on top. You have to operate within your personal truth and you will have to use your best judgement.

Gray Rock: Gray Rock is primarily a way of encouraging a psychopath, a stalker or other emotionally unbalanced person, to lose interest in *you*. It differs from "No Contact" in that you don't overtly try to avoid contact with these emotional vampires. Instead, you allow contact, but only give boring, monotonous responses so that the parasite must go elsewhere for their supply of drama. In essence, you *become* a gray rock. When contact with you is *consistently* unsatisfying for the psychopath, his or her mind is re-trained to expect boredom rather than drama. Psychopaths are addicted to drama and they can't stand to be bored. With time, he will find a new person to provide drama and he will find himself drawn to you less and less often. Eventually, they just slither away to greener pastures. Gray Rock is a way of training the psychopath to view you as an unsatisfying pursuit — you bore him and he can't stand boredom. *(Publication: 180 Rule, The Gray Rock Method of Dealing with Psychopaths, copyright: 2012)*

Canned Responses: Canned responses should be a staple item in your arsenal and can be used to further bore the daylights out of the narcissist in your life. The desired outcome of using canned responses is the same as the Gray Rock method. I recommend that my clients keep between 5-10 canned responses at their fingertips at all times to be used in a variety of situations. Here are a handful of examples of canned responses that you can use – many of these shared by clients or followers:

- If my ex-husband were to send me an email falsely accusing me of sending my 5-year old son to school without a jacket in 40-degree weather, my response would be, "Your accusation is false and your attempt to portray me in a negative light is noted. I do not agree with your representation of the situation."

- A general attack on my parenting would simply be answered with, "Your attempt to portray me in a negative light is noted."

- Any request to violate a court order by proposing a schedule change would be met with, "I intend to follow the court order from (date) exactly as it is written," or, "I intend to follow the court order from Judge Smith exactly as it is written." Citing the actual Judge will show that you honor their orders if the issue is addressed in future court proceedings.

- Misrepresentation of an incident or event can be combatted with, "Your recollection of the incident at the soccer field is very different from mine."

- If your ex is ignoring time-sensitive requests such as approval to sign the children up for an extracurricular activity, this is what I recommend: "If I do not hear from you by 5pm on January 23, I will be left to assume that you agree and we will proceed as outlined in the email above."

Courtesy: When I use the word, "courtesy," I am not recommending you treat your ex-narcissist the same way you would treat your sweet, elderly neighbor. I am suggesting that for purposes of your own best interest (and that of your children), you refrain from suggesting the narcissist take a giant leap off the nearest tall building and instead, use common courtesy in the same way you would in a professional, business-like email. My email signature was automated to say,

"Thank you, Tina" so I didn't have to actually type those words out. If your narcissist took your child to buy a pair of shoes, you may want to begin your next email by saying, "Thanks for picking up Chelsea's shoes- I appreciate that." With the examples given, I believe there are some narcissists who are not candidates for this type of interaction. Ultimately, you need to operate within your truth and this suggestion is not an option for many of my clients so, "No, Tina...I am covering my ears and tuning you out!" is an acceptable answer here.

Rule #4: Utilizing Separate Emails or Our Family Wizard

You should not be receiving emails from the Narcissist on your personal email account. Create an email account specifically for non-emergency communication with the narcissist and better yet, begin using Talking Parents (free) or Our Family Wizard (paid annual subscription). If this is not already a court order in your case, please consider requesting it. Part of my custody evaluation in 2013 included an investigation into Parental Alienation claims against me. One of the things that ended up saving me was the Our Family Wizard program.

In 2012, I had sent Seth a very polite email requesting that we begin using Our Family Wizard (OFW). Seth declined stating that it was too expensive. I went ahead and purchased my license *and his*. While I could not afford to do it at the time, it was the best $198 I've ever spent. In the evaluation, I was able to show my attempts to co-parent with Seth. Purchasing his license demonstrated that I was willing to go above and beyond to co-parent with this madman. While I didn't purchase it for this reason, it ended up helping me tremendously. After I purchased his license, I began utilizing the program by adding the visitation schedule into the calendar along with the children's events, receipts and notifications. My decision to buy OFW for both of us and then, to utilize it to keep him informed shot his parental alienation claims out of the water once and for all. While OFW does have a phone app, I do not recommend installing this on your phone. You do not need the added temptation to check the messages at midnight and you do not need the automatic notification feature to "beep" and notify you of a message while you are out to coffee with your boss or co-worker.

Rule #5: Choosing Your Battles

"Choose your battles wisely. After all, life isn't measured by how many times you stood up to fight. It's not winning battles that makes you happy, but it's how many times you turned away and chose to look into a better direction. Life is too short to spend it on warring. Fight only the most, most, most important ones, let the rest go." — C. Joy Bell

In the beginning of my case, I was ready for battle at every turn. I was under constant attack and consumed by the injustice that my children and I were facing. As someone who is honest and ethical, I place a great deal of value on truthfulness but discovered that perjury in Family Court is an everyday practice with no consequences. Although I kept documenting every lie, I became selective about the ones that needed to be placed in front of the court. I quickly realized that this is a "he said - she said" battle and I was dealing with a good liar so solid facts and documentation were critical.

Before I understood NPD, I begged Seth to be on time (or show up at all) and to keep the phone calls coming because I wanted consistency for my daughters. Looking back, I would have simply noted his failure to show up or call in my log and left it at that, going on to enjoy a peaceful, Seth-free day. I would have set specific days and times to work on my court case versus allowing binders and paperwork to take up residency on my bedroom floor. I allowed this battle to be a constant and never ending project. I hadn't learned to compartmentalize the chaos. If I could rewind, I would have continued to document everything, but I would have carefully chosen the battles that were worth fighting.

I encourage you to break your battle into categories. Begin to really examine each part of your battle and carefully decide where you are going to put your energy. Choose your battles wisely - continue to document everything, but keep your focus on the things that will really matter in court. If you aren't sure which issues will matter to your particular Judge, spend time in the courtroom as an observer and get to know your Judge like the back of your hand. Educating and desensitizing yourself to your local court system and judges will help you to pick your battles wisely.

Rule #6: Taking Control of Communication

Depending on the age of your children, I often recommend that my clients send updates to the other party weekly (infants/younger children), bi-monthly (school-age children) or monthly (teenagers). This does not pertain to everyone, but if you are facing alienation claims in court or out of court, I highly recommend it. Younger children require more updates while older children require less frequent communication. I suggest using a very templated (aka boring) email that shows your attempts at co-parenting and it also allows you to take control of the communication which the narcissist will hate. Each time, I recommend keeping the format the same (just cut/paste) and if a certain subject header doesn't pertain that week (or month), I just write, "N/A." Here is an example of a monthly email – please feel free to adjust as needed for your own use:

Dear Seth,

In an attempt to co-parent in a more productive manner and in an effort to streamline communication and avoid the numerous back and forth messages, I will begin sending one email per month (1st day of each month) to keep you informed and up to date on Piper and Sarah.

Academics: Sarah has a mid-term on December 14th and parent conferences are in January. I will send you the dates and times when I am notified.

Extracurricular: Soccer season begins on November 12th – I have attached the game schedule and unless I hear back from you by October 1st, I will assume you are in agreement with signing them up for the season.

Health: N/A

Misc: N/A

Financial: I did not receive child support for November. Please advise when I should expect it.

Moving forward, I will only be checking emails once or twice per week so any emergency communication should come to my (cell or text). Thank you, Tina

Please note: the purpose of this weekly/monthly update is to reclaim your sanity, take your power back and paint yourself in a positive light with the court. You are *not* sending these emails because we have any hope of this communication "changing" the narcissist or making him/her more reasonable. Hit "send" and let go of attachments and expectations. Sending the template email on time each week (or month) allows you to take control of the communication. Set specific times in your day planner to check your email but do not, by any means, check your email day and night, seven days a week. This is giving the narcissist way too much power. I personally checked each Tuesday and Thursday morning and no more than that.

Learning how to properly communicate with a narcissist is a huge step in taking your power back. Dealing with a narcissist is a constant battle and one that can easily consume you. There is no blanket answer for how to choose your battles and with every case, there are multiple variables involved. Some of those variables involve the players in the equation such as judges, attorneys, therapists, GALs, etc. and other variables including the ages of your children and the specifics on your case. It would be easy to jump into battle-mode and stay there permanently, but we don't want to do that.

CHAPTER 4

KNOWING YOUR TRUTH

If you have followed my work, I am a heavy promoter and advocate of "knowing your truth." While it may sound cliché, it is a powerful cliché that warrants closer examination and personal implantation. I remember emailing my Aunt Bev late one night in tears. Seth had delivered another doozy of an email that attacked my intelligence and education, specifically, the fact that I did not have a college degree hanging on my wall. It had been one email after another and I was feeling beaten down.

Deep down, I knew that even if I did have a college degree adorning my office wall, Seth would attack the college that I attended or he would say that I slept with my professors to earn the degree. He would claim that the document was counterfeit or that I had cheated my way through college. The bottom line was that Seth would find a way to attack me at every turn because this behavior is how the narcissist receives his feed or high.

My Aunt Bev has been my rock for my entire life. She has guided me and supported me through the dark times and cheered me on through the good times. She is very realistic and has never led me down the wrong path. When I am down, I can count on her to either give me a loving but swift kick in the ass or to pick me up and dust me off. When I received the latest crippling email from Seth attacking my educational background, this is the email that I received back from my very wise Aunt:

> *Tina- You know the truth about you but you haven't let it become your foundation yet. Let the truth be your foundation— then nothing anyone says will affect you. Learn from the "Three Little Pigs." Build your "house" so that no one can destroy it. Be strong in what you know.*
>
> *I suggest that you build your foundation by building a list (and emotionally absorbing it) of truths about Tina. Then do a list of lies about Tina. Be confident of both. That is what you need to do in your mind and in court—show what an ugly, evil, nasty person he is and how his lies make him uglier. You are a strong, healthy, loving, kind, beautiful, intelligent woman and an amazing mom. Period. Own it. I love you with all my heart. - Auntie*

Those were the words that I needed to hear in that moment and from that point on, I built my life and my court case on my truth. I stood firm on that foundation and no matter how hard the big, bad wolf blew, he could not knock my house down. I made a list of the truths about Tina and I made a list about the lies about Tina. I absorbed them and I built my confidence upon "the truth about Tina." This simple exercise allowed me to regain my power and I never looked back.

Truths about Tina: I am an amazing mother. I am a loyal, loving friend and partner. I have a joyful, happy spirit rooted deeply in gratitude. My heart is pure and kind. I am intelligent both in mind and in emotional intelligence. My education, while unconventional, was earned as a successful entrepreneur and I am proud of all I have accomplished.

Lies about Tina: I do not have Lupus nor am I suffering from psychosis. I have never cheated on anyone let alone while I was married. While my mother may have been bi-polar, I am not nor do I suffer from any type of mental instability. I am not nor have I ever struggled with any type of addiction to alcohol. Heck, due to the addiction issues in my marriage and family of origin, I am afraid of being addicted to Jelly Beans! I am not deceitful, manipulative or vindictive. I am not trying to prevent my children from having a relationship with their father, I am however warranted in my efforts to protect them mentally and physically during their time with their father.

I encourage you to create a list of your truths and a list of the lies about you. Be crystal clear in each list and build your foundation on these facts. Let the truth be your foundation. If you know your truth and are confident in your truth, it will be much more difficult to rattle you. Carry your list with you and memorize it. You can also take this a step further and make a list of truths about the narcissist in your life. Reference this list often and think to yourself, "consider the source."

PART TWO

CHAPTER 5

THE SETH VAULT

While it's one thing to read *about* Narc-ish, it's another to actually read Narc-ish. In 2014, I was granted permission by a Family Court Judge to close a very painful chapter in my life. When I heard the Judge actually call Seth a sociopath, I was in utter disbelief. When that same Judge allowed the girls and I to forge ahead in complete peace with no further contact with the monster who had terrorized us for years, my head was spinning.

It would have been so easy for me to run away from anything having to do with NPD and the Family Court System, or would it? There are so many people around the world struggling to make sense of the dark path they are on. I remember feeling so alone in this journey and never want anyone else to feel that way. I feel that everything happens for a reason and I read a quote last year that really helped me to understand the journey I was given, "You have been assigned this mountain to show others it can be moved."

While I was in the midst of this battle, I couldn't understand what I had done to deserve the trials I was facing. Looking back, I now understand why. If I can give one other person hope or inspiration, or make another person feel less alone, my work is complete. When I decided to write the *Narc Decoder*, I knew that I would be forced to open a vault door that I had been so ecstatic to close. Once I embarked on the journey of writing this book, I had to step away multiple times because reliving the insanity became too overwhelming for my healing soul. At one point, I developed an eye twitch that lasted for weeks and the nightmares returned. This time, the difference was that when I woke up, it was just a dream and it was no longer my life. For that, I am eternally grateful.

This chapter contains the actual messages that haunted me through this six-year journey. In the past, I've described this as a never-ending rollercoaster with a madman at the controls. Rereading these messages, that's exactly what it was. Over time, I became more empowered through education and comradery with others on the battlefield. I learned to compartmentalize the chaos and I learned to stand in my truth. I chose joy and found it to be my path to healing.

Surviving this battle goes against everything the narcissist had planned for you. As Beyoncé once said, "I'm a Survivor" and my friend, so are you. Now it's time to open the vault doors.

Please note that for your viewing pleasure, we kept the poor grammatical structure of Seth's original message intact for authenticity.

Narc Decoder #1

<u>Background</u>: We were in the beginning stages of separation. We had just lost both of our businesses and Seth secured a position in Northern California. I was job hunting and our daughters were both in preschool but out of school for the summer which made working very difficult. I had confronted him about his new home which was a mini-mansion on the

bluffs of Pacifica, California. Meanwhile, I was struggling to buy groceries. At the time, I did not understand narcissism and his quest for grandiose living was both dumbfounding and infuriating to me.

Original Message:

Tina - You decided to get a divorce. This is all you. You just don't get it. I went to college. I got a 4.0 through high school because I studied hard and was disciplined. I worked my ass off my whole youth. I would study 40 hours for tests in college. Now I have a semi-stable job because of that effort. And you want me to live in college house and slum it now that I am 35 years old. Forget it!

You partied through high school, played hooky and didn't care. Now you are making excuse after excuse about why you can't work. Well you are going to have to work. That is the bottom line. You should go back into retail - weren't you a Gold Star achiever in customer service or something? - Seth

"Snap, fizzle, pop" and out comes the decoded email:

Tina - You originally asked for a divorce in 2008 but I talked you into staying…I'm smooth like that! I then walked out on you and the girls when the marriage therapist wanted me to take a psych eval – how dare he see through the façade I was trying to sell him! I am irate that you refused to take me back after I spent six months dating new women (maybe a few men but that can never be proven) only to discover that my life at home wasn't so bad after all. New women don't want to put up with my bizarre, feminine, drunken behavior like you did for so many years. Damn them!

I know it's been a while since I rubbed your nose in my shiny college degree and degraded you. Do you miss it as much as I do? I love making you feel bad about yourself so I jump at any opportunity to tell you how great I am and what a low-life you are.

Since you are angry that I rented an ocean-front palace while you can't afford food for the girls, I am going to use this opportunity to turn things around and tell you how much better I am than you. Peasants like you don't deserve to eat. I *need* to spend money in bars each week. Priorities here, Tina! I don't understand why you don't just lock the kids in a closet and find a job! Furthermore, I think you should scrap your ten years of experience running profitable businesses to take a minimum-wage job in retail. That would give me more topics to degrade you with while talking to my family. Did I mention that all of my family members are highly educated? It's always worth repeating if it makes you cringe. Did it make you cringe? Please say it did? - Seth

Suggested response:

Nothing. Nada. Zilch. No response needed.

<u>Note</u>: Engaging on an email of this type would provide Seth with his narcissistic feed and prolong the attacks.

###

Narc Decoder #2

<u>Background:</u> Separated for six months and Seth found out that I had a social life away from him and our marriage. I had just met Glenn (now husband), and we had developed a strong friendship. Despite the fact that he had been dating multiple women for six months, it was unacceptable when the tables were turned.

Original Message:

Tina- First please walk with me through this anecdote. At dusk last night I was running up Montara Mountain which soars thousands of feet above the Pacific Ocean. I was trying to decide what to do as I can't focus on much right now. I have lost everything. Now I have lost my wife too. My foregone conclusion, I caused this by my own pride and lack of caring. Thus I run mountains to deal with the stress of my colossal failure. Painfully enduring an hour of running uphill is my therapy.

On the top ridges, wildlife changes from furry rabbits and songbirds to hawks and big bucks. After enjoying the top for a few minutes I began the descent. At the top as I first careened down the narrow trail, I was startled as right over my head two blue doves in a tree who fluttered away less than five feet from my head. I have never seen doves while running a trail. I continued down and they slowly descended down the valley together. Two blue doves at 2,000 feet above sea level. What does this mean? Well it must mean I must focus on love, forgiveness and apologies now.

I have been full of pride and driven by success. To you, I have failed to deliver the level of affection you deserve. I am actually very emotional but I don't like sharing my feelings as I think this shows weakness or lack of masculinity for some reason. I was afraid of counseling. I was afraid of the counselor chipping away at the shell that I used to plow forward at the expense of myself and the family. Well, I know I lost myself in those years of running a business. I feel like I put on a façade and became a different person over the last 6 years…and for what? A big house on the hill filled with designer furniture. Burn it to the ground, I don't care.

Looking back, I was happiest in my life when we were together. Yes, there was an inner drive in me that pushed for success on all levels. But I truly have the best memories of my life when we were together in love on vacations, Jamaica, Hawaii especially in 2001 and 2004. The highest time of my life I think was when we were living in Marin in our little 1940s home. This summer when we stayed in the little Lake cottage in New Hampshire, Piper loved that little house, and said so. That touched me. The children care about closeness and the love within our family. Bottom line.

So here it is. I have been a total dick. I should have just let it all go and get back to living life. I should have apologized more. I should have stopped spending beyond our means. I finally have a little taste of life like it was back in Marin again. And enjoying life, the outdoors, new experiences with the girls, flying a kite for the first time, watching Piper and Sarah playing with friends at the beach, or Sarah covering herself head to toe in sand at Pismo Beach—this is what life is about. This is life for me.

Work should cover food, rent and offer some free money to find new ways to enjoy life. Work over the past 6 years has consumed me and swallowed me alive. I think our counselor failed to get past the money issues as they were so Titanic. He didn't give us any concrete 1-10 steps on making headway. That five months of counseling totally failed because he was the wrong guy. I will go to any counselor of your choice as long as it is less than $50/hour. I will pay for it by delivering newspapers at 4 am if I need to. I will make a 180-degree attitude change. I will embrace and follow the processes and steps in these books Emotional Fitness for Couples, What You Feel You Can Heal, Seven Levels of Intimacy. You can continue racing away and discovering yourself every weekend. The girls and I are having lots of fun. Only difference would be I would get a hug when you leave and return. I think I still remember how to do that. I want you to discover yourself, to grow independently of me. To live simply and enjoy life. You deserve it.

Most importantly, you have now said everything that has been on your chest that normally would have come out in counseling. I too have said everything that has been on my chest. The most recent comment about your weight was inappropriate. You do look as good as you looked 5 years ago when we raced off to Jamaica. I don't know if that is because you are tanning, lost 10 pounds, are wearing your old clothes....I don't know what it is but you are hot. Maybe just being away from you made me realize how stupid I have been. I was so naïve to push you away *and alienate you when times became tougher.*

Regardless of your decision, I forgive you. If you go through six more months of counseling with me and it doesn't work, you can keep everything. I don't care about the stuff, the furniture, it's useless. This is your decision to accept the "me" of seven years ago, stripped to nothing, with no more than the heart and desire to change…or move on in your life alone. The choice is yours. PS Waldorf Couples Counseling Resort is $99 a night in Arizona on Priceline. Love (hopefully), Seth

"Snap, fizzle, pop" and out comes the decoded email:

Tina- First, it would be helpful if you'd swallow this nice concoction of tranquilizers that I've prepared so I can brainwash you into staying with me. Eh hmmm….let the poetry begin…it's worked like a charm hundreds of times before! At dusk last night I was running up Montara Mountain which soars thousands of feet above the Pacific Ocean. Have I flexed for you lately? No, no…that was the mirror I was flexing for. Back to my story (this is the good part…the part where I play the victim), I am having a difficult time as I've lost all of my material possessions and control over you. For the purpose of emotionally scamming you, I'm going to take the blame for all of the losses we've faced but for the record, I blame the loan department of the bank for my failure. How dare they not buy into my scheme and float me another $200K! Those assholes!

On the top ridges, there were cute fuzzy bunnies and songbirds chirping your name… "Tina…Tina….take Seth back…tweedle dee…" It was SO cute! There were also doves (not really but I know they hold special meaning to you and that you will see this as a sign we should be together. Anyway, back to my story.) Two blue doves in a tree fluttered away less than five feet from my head. I have never seen doves while running a trail because I'm usually too busy checking out my own calf muscles. I continued down and the imaginary doves slowly descended down the valley together. Two blue doves at 2000 feet above sea level! What does this mean? Well it must mean that you should take me back – get it? WE are the doves! Duh!

I am and always have been full of pride and driven to use and abuse others for my own success. I have zero emotions which makes me sound inhuman so mums the word! I was afraid of going to counseling for fear of someone chipping away at me or asking me to take a psych evaluation. Looking back, I was most happy in my life when we were together. I truly have the best memories of my life when I was pretending to be in love with you on vacations such as Jamaica and Hawaii. Especially from 2000 - 2004 because we didn't have kids and you only weighed 100lbs! Those were the days! The highest time of my life I think was when we were living in Marin in our little 1940s home. I really miss having a bubbly blonde girl on my arm and if you notice, the best times (for me) were pre-children. I hate going places alone because I am so socially awkward. I miss having you as my shield!

Is the tranquilizer kicking in yet? I'm about to go deeper by telling you that I want the same things you've always wanted – the LITTLE house, the normal cars, and to spend my weekends flying a kite with the kids. I want whatever you want and then, as soon as you are back in my web, I will start spending thousands of dollars a day to impress people who don't even like me with stuff we don't need. We both know that everything I am feeding you right now is bullshit but if the tranquilizer starts to kick in, you may actually believe me!

I think our counselor failed to get past the money issues as they were so Titanic. Let's not talk about the fact that I ran us into debt to the tune of 1.6 million. I think everything was the therapist's fault despite the fact that he has a PhD and was intimately familiar with psychopaths. I think he saw through me – what an epic failure he was! That five months of counseling totally failed because he was the wrong guy!

Please ignore my recent comment about the fact that I haven't been turned on by you in five years. Now, due to the stress of our separation and the fact that you can't hold down food, you do look as good as you looked 5 years ago, pre-children. I don't know if that is because you are tanning, lost 10 pounds, wearing your old clothes? I don't know but now, you are hot and because of that, I want you back! I would love to continue to pull one over on you by luring you to a couples retreat! Interested? Here...have another yummy little tranquilizer! - Seth

Suggested Response:

Ignore.

###

Narc Decoder #3

<u>Background</u>: We had been separated for about six months and were attempting a "nesting agreement" which essentially meant the girls got to sleep in their own beds each night. I stayed in our home with the girls Monday through Friday and Seth returned to the home on the weekends at which time, I would leave for the weekend. Seth's behavior was becoming erratic and frightening especially after I refused his attempt at reconciliation. Concerned about his behavior, I notified him that I was taking the girls to a friend's home and that we would not be honoring his weekend visitation. Because there was no court order in place at this time, I was legally in a position to do this. When Seth arrived at the home for his parenting time, he was irate that we were gone and left three disturbing, highly intoxicated, slurring voicemails on my phone between 10pm and 2am.

Original Message(s):

10pm: Tina- I am going to very clear with you. Its 10pm on Friday night. My daughters should be with me right now. Your behavior over the past six months has proven not only that you are a bad mom but that you are a bad influence on my daughters. If my daughters are not at my house...do you understand this...my house! I pay rent on. I own this house. It's my house. Do you understand that? At 8am tomorrow morning. 8am tomorrow morning Saturday I will be emailing 3,000 people every picture that I have of you and ultimately, Tina you will be wrecked in this community. I do not care. I think you are white trash I think you are a slut. And yes, you can record this.

61

I think you are a slut! Do you understand that? You've slept with three people in three months while we were married and yes, I think you are a slut. And I think that before we got married you had slept with many, many people and I really don't care Tina, all I care about is the influence that I can impart on my daughters so that they have a good life without your influence. I think you have zero ability to impart a good perspective on them and I will tell you right now that if my daughters aren't sitting here at 8am in the morning during the time that I am supposed to be with them then you will be ruined in this community and I will have no regrets for sending an email to 3,000 people of the pictures of you…your own actions while we were married. 8am tomorrow…have my daughters here or you are DONE.

2:16am: Tina. There is currently a court order where my daughters are at MY home that I pay for from 10pm on Friday until 8am on Tuesday. The problem here is that you have not delivered my daughters to my house. I will be issuing an Amber Alert in the morning if my daughters are not at my house. I will be calling the police department if my daughters are not at my house. You are on thin ice, Tina and I have a list of 3000 local business people that I will email pictures of your infidelity and sleeping with three different men if my daughters are not here. Do you not understand that? If my daughters are not here, I will email 3000 people and show your infidelity and the bottom line Tina, is that you are a bad person. What you've done this far proves that you are a bad person. There is karma in this world and you will just have to deal with that. My daughters will not be influenced by someone who sleeps with 55-year old men for money. Do you understand that? They will NOT be influenced

62

by you. You have until 8am tomorrow morning before your world completely collapses. I want my daughters at my house 8am tomorrow morning...Saturday morning. Take care.

2:32am: Tina- You are a white trash bitch for letting my dog out of the fence. And I'll tell you what Tina. I am going to file a restraining order and you will not be allowed back at this house. Do you understand that? YOU are a LOOSER. Do you understand this? And I am going to prove it in court. You are a looser, your white trash, YOU ARE WHITE TRASH, do you understand this? You have been sleeping with three men in three months and I am going to prove that as well. I just have nothing more to say to you.

"Snap, fizzle, pop" and out comes the decoded email:

Tina- I am highly intoxicated and bat shit crazy which pairs nicely with a fat dollop of delusional thinking and extra sprinkles of rage. I just left five minutes' worth of voice mails for you to take to the court and prove that I am a drunk lunatic. I am going to sit here in the dark wearing my whitey-tighty underwear and downing shots of tequila while making up scenarios about you cheating. I am also going to throw out whatever other bizarre accusations that I pull out of my ass. - Seth

Suggested Response:

No response.

Note: I heard all of these messages when I woke up on Saturday morning and I was terrified. I took my daughters to the local women's shelter and filed an emergency hearing for exclusive use of our home. The order was granted and true to narcissistic fashion, Seth violated the order and entered my home 24 hours later. True to Family Court fashion, there were no consequences.

Narc Decoder #4

<u>Background</u>: During a particularly tumultuous time in my custody battle, when Seth was oscillating between regular visits and supervised visits, I refused to meet him at his family's residence because I not only feared Seth but also his older brother and father. While trying to come to an agreement on meeting locations, I suggested the police department.

Original Message:

Tina- None of the men in my family have committed an act of harm towards a woman. It's just delusional that you have such fear of me. I have previously thought about having the exchange at the Police Department. The police department is a scary setting for the children and there is no reason for it. When I was a kid Police made me nervous. You think after you've dragged me to court for three years over nonsense and exaggerations, I would risk yelling at you or harming you, it's just preposterous, Tina. I am not going to do anything to hurt you. I will compromise and agree to meet you at the park. - Seth

<u>"Snap, fizzle, pop" and out comes the decoded email:</u>

Tina- I have not yet committed a serious act of harm towards a woman, but I am starting to worry about the fact that three different women have now testified that they live in fear due to my instability, stalking and passive-aggressive threats. Since I have had multiple run-ins with law enforcement over the past ten years, police make me nervous and cause increased anxiety. I would prefer that we do not meet near a police station. Thank you, Seth

Suggested response:

We will see you at the court-ordered meeting location at 9am. Thank you, Tina.

###

Narc Decoder #5

Background: One of 100 random text messages sent to me each day in 2009.

Original Message:

Tina - The most tragic part is what you are doing and have done to damage the girls. You will have men you date screw you over after they use for a few months. That's all you are good for. When you remarry, the next guy will cheat on you. 58% of men cheat and you are attracted to that type. Good luck with your life. - Seth

"Snap, fizzle, pop" and out comes the decoded email:

Tina - The most tragic part is what I have done to you and the girls. I am moving on and will begin screwing women and dumping them as soon as they catch wind of who I am. My goal is to dump them before they dump me because my ego can only handle so much! I hate the fact that you are capable of moving on and learning from your experiences with me. The thought of you meeting a normal man and having a healthy relationship eats at me every day and every night. I want you to fail miserably at everything including future relationships. This way, I can blame you for the demise of every relationship you have – including ours. – Seth

Suggested Response:

Ignore.

###

Narc Decoder #6

Background: At the start of our battle in 2009, Seth had weekend visitation that began at 9am on Friday and ended on Sunday at 6pm. I had discovered that he was driving without a license and insisted that his mom provide transportation. He knew that I had plans to go out of town with friends.

Original Message:

Tina- I need email confirmation tonight that you won't bring up license in court, nor quiz Piper about our time, who drove etc. or I won't be there at 9am Friday. -Seth

"Snap, fizzle, pop" and out comes the decoded email:

Tina- I am so arrogant and above rules that I would actually put something like this in writing. You are so stupid to insist that I have a driver's license like everyone else in the world. I am above all of those little paupers with a license. I would like you to put it in writing that I am allowed to drive unlicensed and that you won't hold that against me in court. Despite the IQ that I brag about, I am really pretty stupid as you can see by this email. You also need to promise that you won't ask Piper about the bizarre things that occur during my parenting time which often leave her distraught. If you don't agree to these things, I will cancel yet another visit. Actually, I would love to cancel the visit because I know you have plans and I hate that you are moving forward with your life. -Seth

Suggested Response:

Seth- You cannot drive the girls without a license. That is illegal. I will contact your mom to ensure that she is available to transport the girls during your parenting time. -Tina

###

Narc Decoder #7

Background: At Hallmark, they have cards in a category called "Just Because." Through this journey, I found that narcissists love to send their own version of these cards in the form of Narc-ish text messages, emails and voicemails. They seem to come out of the blue and usually involve large amounts of alcohol or periods of time where they are alone and spinning. This was one of many "Just Because" text messages that came through my phone.

Original Message:

Tina- The beauty of my karma is that I have had mine delivered. I have lost everything. Wish you well, Tina. -Seth

"Snap, fizzle, pop" and out comes the decoded email:

Tina- I get my jollies by threatening you with karma. For me, it's like mind masturbation. Oh how I love it! It's a way for me to threaten your life without crossing legal limits. What I am really trying to say is, I hope to see you in a dark alley where I will promptly slit your throat. Wish you well, Tina. Sleep tight! -Seth

Suggested Response:

None.

###

Narc Decoder #8

Background: Seth was obsessed with my looks and weight during our marriage and post-separation. He emailed me and texted me about it almost daily. I attended a concert with friends on my non-parenting weekend in 2009 and received this random message at 2am.

Original Message:

So, standing next to stick-thin Traci and Taren at the concert, did you successfully get hit on by as many men? Last night was the time to meet your 20lb weight loss goal. All I could assume is you were headed in the same direction so many moms go down. Shame. Add that to the venomous talk that you are accusing me of. I just wasn't attracted to you anymore. I didn't put effort in the last 18-months because your tone in talk became more resentful. Plus, you were getting fatter and fatter. Immature maybe, but true. -Seth

"Snap, fizzle, pop" and out comes the decoded email:

Tina - I am sitting home alone drinking heavily while the girls are tucked in bed sleeping. I actually snuck out and left them home alone again because at 2 and 4-years old, they sleep pretty deeply and didn't even know I was at the bars until 2am. Fooled them! I hate that you are thinner now and that other people may look at you and compliment you. Have I mentioned how disgusted I was by your pregnancies? When I hired you…errr…I mean, married you, I expected you to stay 115 lbs at all times. I hate that you started standing up to me during the last 18 months of our marriage and putting boundaries in place. You were supposed to stay quiet and do as I said just like my mom did while I was growing up. P.S. I hate you. – Seth

Suggested Response:

Ignore.

###

Narc Decoder #9

<u>Background:</u> Seth was myopically focused on my wedding ring and had been since his original proposal. In his attempted prenuptial agreement, he actually wanted it back if the marriage didn't last for at least 10 years. The original cost for the ring was $11,000. Seth sent this message about three weeks before he formally filed for divorce. We had been separated for almost 6 months.

Original Message:

Tina- Would you be willing to trade your wedding ring back to me for $5,000 within 30 days? When I get paid my bigger check, I can give you cash. You see, I will unlikely ever be able to buy a ring like this for 10 or more years. I financed that ring on a Nordstrom credit card. I will never be able to do that again. Besides that, you know the history of that ring and you will never wear it again. The thing is YOU will be engaged in 1 to 5 years unquestionably. Some rich guy will sweep you off your feet when you really start dating again. I don't know when you will be serious about someone again and it kills me to think about. I am going to be broke for a long time. I will be unable to afford a way to propose to someone when I do regain my strength and want to date.

It really is scary being single for me. I hate socializing alone. Socializing is your thing and that is why I was drawn to you. You gave me energy and without you: I have none. With no time to date, and no money, I am in a downward spiral. All my money is swallowed up by this dual household. At least this would help me have hope for the future. – Seth

"Snap, fizzle, pop" and out comes the decoded email:

Tina – Material items have always held more meaning to me than real relationships. I obsessively spent months and months scouting out the perfect diamond and I loved that ring more than I ever loved you. I want to be able to use your ring to propose to my next unsuspecting victim however, I will insist she sign a pre-nup because I will be wearing that ring to my own funeral one day. It really is scary being single for me – this is probably the only honest thing that's come out of my mouth. I am in a downward, alcohol-induced spiral and having your ring would comfort me….and give me hope that if I played one girl for ten years, I will surely find another to play! You can also be sure that if I give you a check for the ring, it will bounce like a rubber ball. Boing! Boing! Boing! –Seth

Suggested Response:

None.

###

Narc Decoder #10

Background: Narcissists often pick a "golden child" and in our case, it fluctuated between both girls in the beginning but after Sarah's seizures at 10-months old, he deemed her genetically flawed (my fault, of course) and Piper became his obsession.

71

Original Message:

Tina- I am reading a book about people who are defined as genius. Piper might be one. Please have her read nightly. I'll send you published papers if you'd like to attest to this. This has nothing to do with me. You are an idiot if you refuse to cultivate Piper or Sarah through extracurricular education. You lack so much…and it's because of your upbringing and lack of cultivation. Lacking culture or a groomed skill. Just looks. So sad. -Seth

"Snap, fizzle, pop" and out comes the decoded email:

Tina- I am reading a book about people who are defined as genius and Piper, receiver of my superior genes may very well be one. While I understand she is only five, I'd like you to begin forcing college-level books on her. It may be helpful to read these books to her while she sleeps along with the nations top medical journals. Hypnosis is powerful and the mind can absorb messages even while sleeping. I'll send you published papers but you probably won't understand what they mean. This has everything to do with me because if she is a genius, I will take full credit but if she isn't, it's obviously your fault. You are an idiot if you refuse to comply with my demands on cultivating our three-year-old and five-year-old through forced extracurricular education that will leave their little heads spinning. I lack so much…love, honesty, empathy, and I hate that you have all three. Therefore, I will put you down and degrade you any chance I get. You are stupid for leaving me. My children better turn out to be geniuses or you'll never hear the end of this! -Seth

Suggested Response:

Seth- I read to the girls every night. I will continue to follow recommendations on reading materials from Piper's kindergarten teacher. -Tina

Narc Decoder #11

<u>Background</u>: The cost of my health insurance increased to the point that I could no longer afford to cover myself and the girls. Due to my autoimmune disease, my out of pocket costs alone, not covered by insurance was over $500 per month and as a single mom, it was more than I could afford. Once I received notification that Seth was employed after a six-month job loss, I cancelled my family policy. True to fashion, this gave Seth ammunition to email me with.

Original Message:

Tina- Why did you cancel the health insurance for the girls? With my loss of a job last year due to various factors including your constant harassment and vexatious litigation against me, you did a good job providing insurance for a few months. Why did you cancel our daughters' insurance? I would have thought you'd follow the court order to maintain health insurance for the children.

Albeit, you have not once in 4 years done anything to help ensure that our daughters could have a normal healthy father-daughter relationship with me, their father. Instead, you didn't

show up at countless scheduled visitations because I didn't notify you precisely at 10:59 AM. You knew I was waiting, yet you refused to let me spend a few precious hours with the girls. You are obsessed with "destroying me." Through your blog, you are publicly demonstrating that you are mentally unstable in the community.

You are proving you are vengeful, selfish and uninterested in how much damage you are causing the girls for your own "ego boost." I am going to seek damages to my reputation and my parent's career options. This is inevitable if you continue your libel, slander and defamation. Or just use your free will, do what's in the best interest of (the girls) reputations now and when they're teenage girls and stop all of your defamation and libel.

Tina your desire for fame and money is obviously more important to you than preserving our daughter's sanctity and privacy. I doubt your book will generate any profit, but the point is the girls are going to be emotionally damaged forever by your book/blog. What if I walked around calling you names and saying you're bi-polar. How would they feel about themselves when they heard their mom has more than a few screws loose?

You have not once in 4 years done anything to help ensure our daughters could have a relationship of love and nurture with me, their father. You don't tell me about their performances, you had Glenn bring them to a father-daughter ball and you make Piper feel rewarded when she informs you of anything negative. I am not "disturbed" nor am I a "Narcissist," a "psychopath" or "sick." I have been successful in my past with education and business but my only interest now is the girls, and ensuring they make it through college with a healthy and free attitude to enjoy life and the challenges.

Tina you went to a continuation high school. You barely finished high school. You're a good fiction writer, that I'll give you. But you have zero training in psychology. You have the audacity to write, "As you know, I was successful in obtaining new parenting evaluation at our last hearing," Tina you asked that my daughters were limited to see me on Saturdays (with a supervisor present). Your filing an FL-300 "Request for an Order" was to take the children away from me completely. Your blog is a conundrum of crafted and intricate lies.

I asked as Item #1 for a Custody Evaluation because our children need a mentally stable parent in their lives. You're clearly demonstrating pathological patterns of delusion with no Interest in the truth; with no interest on right and wrong; nor how ethically to do what is right for our daughters.

You want money and profit from a delusional fictional narrative in your own (quite possibly clinically bipolar) mind. I am deeply concerned about your mental stability now that I have read your entire blog. It's disturbing on many levels. I am most concerned now about how our children, Piper initially and soon, Sarah's emotional damage will manifest upon exposure to their Mom's words about the Dad they love just as much as you Tina.

You have no idea how negatively this will affect our children. This is no "battle" as you say. It's not about putting on "big girl panties" and "fighting" as you state on your blog. This is *not delusion or fiction Tina, it is about two children whose own sense of self is reliant on a healthy relationship with their father and mother. Their own self-esteem is from both of us Tina. Let them be themselves and decide for themselves Tina.*

I am pleading with you to stop your little ego feed from the blog, go back to earning an income and move on in your life. Stop obsessing over what gym I work out at, where I live, what girlfriend I may have 220 miles from where my daughters reside, and get on with your own life. -Seth

"Snap, fizzle, pop" and out comes the decoded email:

Tina- I love when you give me a reason to email you! Not that I need a reason to crawl out from under my barstool and ridicule you but thanks to the change in health insurance plans, I actually have a legitimate reason. Truth be told...wait, who am I fooling? I've never told the truth! Ha! Anyway, back to the whole health insurance issue. I got fired last year because apparently, they don't like it when you are drunk during work hours, arrogant during all hours, talk down to your boss, don't make sales goals and fail to show up to client meetings. Of course, that's all your fault. I love to twist things. I can make anything your fault!

Albeit (does that word make me sound important? I am, dammit!), you have not once lied for me in 4 years to help ensure that our daughters and I could pretend to have a normal healthy father-daughter relationship. Instead, you didn't show up at countless scheduled visitations just because I violated court orders. You knew I was praying to the porcelain God and still drunk at 10am yet you are obsessed with holding me accountable and I hate it. Through your blog, you are publicly demonstrating that I am mentally unstable. You need to stop immediately. Do you hear me? If we were still married, this would be the point when I'd grab your wrist and squeeze it to show that I really mean business. I MEAN BUSINESS, TINA!

You are proving that I am vengeful, selfish and uninterested in the girls. I use them for my own ego boost. I am going to seek damages to the reputation that I ruined on my own accord and for my parents' lack of career options which stem from my dad being known as the, "pervert principal." People take rumors like that so seriously. This lawsuit is inevitable if you continue to tell the truth about us. Are my threats working? Are you scared yet? Shaking?

My desire for alcohol, grandiose living and money is obviously more important to me than preserving a relationship with my daughters. I hope your book does not generate any profit. I hope you fail at everything you do. The girls are going to be emotionally damaged by my actions and behavior without you shining a spotlight on me. Does it bother you that I walk around calling you names and saying that you're bi-polar? I hope it eats at you. How will the girls feel when they discover from first-hand experience that their dad has more than a few nuts, bolts and screws loose?

As you know, I have no ability to love or nurture anyone and this is your fault also. I hate that you have mounds and mounds of documentation showing your attempts to communicate performances and events with me. The thing that pisses me off most of all is that when I stood the girls up for their Father-Daughter ball, you sprung into action and tried to get my brother to take them. When he couldn't do it, you had the audacity to have Glenn take them! I am SO pissed about this. If I want them to sit home and cry, how dare you prevent it from happening! I'm also madder than hell that Piper feels safe to tell you about my abusive behavior. That kid needs to learn to keep her mouth shut.

I am incredibly "disturbed" and I am a narcissist, a psychopath and one sick little puppy! Have I reminded you lately about my successes in business? I defrauded people all over the county, took my little brother for almost $100,000, lost our house and stripped my parents of their life savings and retirement funds. What a wild, exhilarating ride that was! You, on the other hand, hold on…let me twist reality as I do best. A continuation school! That's it! My new story has you going to a continuation school where you barely graduate because you are *that* stupid. You then slept with the principal to earn your high school diploma. Stupid slut.

I am obsessed with your writing and I print each blog page to send to my mommy. She immediately consoles me and tells me what a bad, bad person you are. My mommy loves me even though my life is a conundrum of crafted and intricate lies. It's disturbing on many levels. You have no idea how negatively this blog will affect me. I am pleading with you to stop your blog and get a job at McDonalds so I can make fun of you. And please, stop hiring PI's to showcase my lies in court. -Seth

Suggested Response:

Seth- The court order states that we must both carry insurance if it is offered at a reasonable cost. The family plan through my job is more than half of my wages. I will let you know if that changes. -Tina

###

Narc Decoder #12

Background: Seth was often a no-show to visitation and little did he know, I was closely watching his movements on social media. The following message was sent at 9pm which was 12 hours before his scheduled parenting time. I had already turned in for the night and received a text message at 11pm advising me to check my email.

Original Message:

Tina- I won't be able to see the girls this weekend. I have a major project due Monday. If it isn't turned in on time I could lose my job. This week I travelled to a university in Oregon and the last two days I was in a training for a new product for 10 hours each day. I couldn't complete my sales plan for the year and its now 18 days past due. I am trying really hard. My job responsibilities are now Alaska, Idaho, Oregon, Utah, Southern California and Northern California. Despite this challenging travel schedule on planes normally wake at 4:30am on Saturday mornings to drive down to see my daughters. Then I get home at 12 am Sunday.

The last 2 weeks in February I missed a 7:00am conference call for our region because I left so late, I didn't even hear my alarm

go off. In fact, I got written up for it as my manager was furious. I propose you work with me here. My job provides you with spending money. If I miss one more meeting, I will be terminated. It would be better if I see the girls 4 days every other week and for 5 days M-F at the beginning of each quarter. This is my last sincere request. I cannot come this weekend. I apologize for the inconvenience this may cause you. I really miss my girls. Perhaps you could move to San Francisco or Marin and make more money and move on with your life in a new area as well. -Seth

"Snap, fizzle, pop" and out comes the decoded email:

Tina- I won't be able to see the girls this weekend because I am going wine tasting in Napa with a group of friends. I am really hoping to get laid and whenever there is a chance to ply women with alcohol, I'm in! I have to use the weekends to drink heavily because my job is on the line due to my excess partying on the weekdays. I have a major project due Monday but I am four months into this job so I expect to be fired any day anyway. People see through me pretty quickly and four months is a pretty good stretch for me! Are you impressed by all the places I travel? Do I sound important? I plan to use these same lines on women this weekend. Actually, I hope they are really young and stupid – much easier to impress if that is the case.

Oh, and despite this impressive travel schedule on airplanes, I stumble home and go to sleep at 4:30am on Saturday mornings. This is why I often stand you and the girls up. I recently missed a 7am conference call and almost lost my job because this partying thing is tough to juggle. It would be great if you could give up your life, rip our children from the only community they've ever known and move to the Bay Area so I can sleep in longer on the weekends. It would be SO much better for me. Will you? Oh! While I am busy cancelling my visit with the girls, I want to propose that I increase my time with them. I really don't care about what's best for them – it would be better for me to see them during the week while they are in preschool and I don't really have to deal with them. It would free me up to party on the weekends. I don't feel bad that I am cancelling on you and leaving you in a huge childcare bind with your job. Not only do I now feel bad, I am laughing hysterically at the thought of you scrambling to find childcare! Won't you please write me back and tell me how much this has affected you? -Seth

Suggested Response:

Nothing. He does not deserve an ounce of my energy nor will I allow him to know that he has caused me a childcare crisis. Breathe, document and move on.

###

Narc Decoder #13

Background: Two years into our divorce and custody battle proceedings, Seth would randomly send the most bizarre emails and text messages. This was one such message that had to do with the legality of our marriage. We were married in Hawaii which according to my research, is one of the 50 states in the United States. In a narcissist's brain, they can really twist reality to the point of it being unrecognizable.

Original Message:

Tina - We had no financial accounts together in over nine years as a couple short of one joint bank account. I don't believe I was really even married to you since we didn't get married in California nor did we think it through. It was basically like a Vegas wedding; and what a mistake! I may be seeking an annulment FYI. Of course if there really is a marriage certificate, that won't affect how the court proceeds but nonetheless it would be more accurate. – Seth

"Snap, fizzle, pop" and out comes the decoded email:

Tina – You were wrong all along– I CAN feel and this email is proof! Right this very moment, I am FEELING drunk and delusional. By the way, this divorce is really putting a damper on my social life and so, I am hoping I can find a loophole to put an end to court. I work in sales and I am skilled at problem solving. I know that I spent months shopping for the perfect diamond and planned the engagement and wedding in advance of our vacation to Maui but I question whether I can convince you and the court to accept my spin on reality. I'm wondering if I would be allowed to serve alcohol in court? It would be so helpful if you and the judge would both agree to get drunk before I launch my sales pitch on the legality of getting married in Hawaii. Hawaii is just like Vegas – neither should qualify as legal marriages…following me here? Drink more, I am. - Seth

Suggested Response:

Just laugh out loud and then call your sister, mom, aunt or best friend to give them a laugh at the expense of the narcissist. That's precisely what I did.

Narc Decoder #14

<u>Background</u>: Seth lost his job after a lengthy, five-month stretch with the same company.

Original Message:

Tina- I got distracted once again with the divorce paperwork and I couldn't perform at 110% and my boss knew it, and his boss knew it. I almost lost my job when the divorce started in 2009. I was on thin ice but turned it around. I take responsibility for my performance in sales, that I can control. Keeping up with paperwork was my downfall, that daily paperwork and reporting requirements I just couldn't stay on top of like I normally could because of the fear of losing my daughters after the legal pleadings I received from you in February.

There is an underlying tide in corporate America to cut people going through divorce, major illnesses, or other life changing events, though H.R. is very careful to find a way to protect themselves from a lawsuit. I saved myself and the income for the family by ignoring you as much as possible and focusing on work and sales performance. I thought I could have one last gasp of air and break from my company. I was wrong.

It would have taken me 160 hours or 4 full weeks of work to properly respond to the 360 odd pages of Exhibits you filed with the court. They were incredulous, full of exaggerations of the truth and painful to read. I have never felt so betrayed by someone yet again. You need to move on with your own life. I couldn't properly and legally complete the paperwork so I tried to hire an attorney. I didn't know how to object to your exhibits which were full of nonsense. You absolutely cost me my job, I couldn't focus when so much was at stake in my personal life. — Seth

"Snap, fizzle, pop" and out comes the decoded email:

Tina- My employer didn't believe that I was as special as I believe I am. They didn't like my over-the-top arrogance, failure to get along with my co-workers, the fact that I drank so much, never showed up for meetings, was constantly hungover and on top of that, had to keep going to court. I got fired. Again. Like anytime I fail at a job, it's your fault. How dare you take me to court and hold me accountable for my actions? If you'd just let me continue to abuse the girls, disregard court orders, fail to show up for visits and drink myself into oblivion, life would be perfect. Stop holding me accountable. I mean it! STOP right now! – Seth

Suggested Response:

None.

###

Narc Decoder #15

<u>Background</u>: Seth was unemployed and in between homes. He was refusing to tell me where the girls would be staying during his parenting time yet the court order required him to give me the address of his residence. In addition, he was requesting a change in the schedule and more time. He didn't have a job, a home, and he was increasingly unstable and had received a recent DUI. I voiced my concern prior to his upcoming visit. The girls had resided in six different locations since our previous court date – just one month earlier.

Original Message:

Tina - You are intolerable!!! Let all of this insipid, bitterness and hostility go. You feel "uncomfortable" because I don't have stability. Blast off Tina!! That is ridiculous!!! There's no difference about how I would care for my daughters. I am concerned about your stability. Talk about delusional instability given that your Mom was diagnosed as having bipolar disorder. I have been very suspicious of your personality change after 2005. More disturbing, I am concerned that my daughters are living with a 58-year old man who I have met only once via car exchange. This is a man whom you had an affair with while we were legally married. I am sure you lied to him back then and said you were already divorced. He could be fine but he is a 58-year old man living with my daughters. Often, these men prey on younger, recently single women with children. That is how children end up molested. – Seth

"Snap, fizzle, pop" and out comes the decoded email:

Tina – HOW DARE YOU ACCUSE ME OF BEING
UNSTABLE?! I AM, I AM, I AM! How dare you point out
your concerns about me? I am intolerable. I am insipid, bitter
and hostile. I am unstable! Just because Sarah and Piper have
been telling you that I mumble and talk to myself while pacing
back and forth, it's none of your business. As you know,
whenever you bring up concerns or point out my flaws, I like
to flip the tables and project my issues onto you. I love to
remind you that your mom was bi-polar. I hate that a stable,
healthy, 44-year old man is in your life. Since he's nine-years
older than you, I am going to inflate his age and cast doubt on
his character in case this is ever submitted to the court. I often
prey on young women so again, I am projecting my own issues.
Just say it's all true and we'll move on. Stop caring about what
happens to the girls while they are in my care. They are MY
possessions and I will do whatever I want with them. Blast off!
- Seth

Suggested Response:

"Seth - I intend to follow Judge Johnson's order
exactly as written. Please forward the address where
the girls will be staying during your parenting time."

###

Narc Decoder #16

Background: After two years on the battlefield of Family
Court, I was awarded sole legal and physical of the girls. I sent
Seth an email to let him know that I was starting Piper in

therapy. I reiterated that I was seeing signs of stress in the girls such as bed wetting, daytime potty accidents, nightmares and anxiety surrounding Seth's parenting time.

Original Message:

Tina- Having Piper in counseling is a good idea. You really need to be careful about Parental Alienation Syndrome or Family Alienation Syndrome. Your "quizzing" Piper about too many things while she is with me. Do not ask her quizzing questions please. My Mom who has a Masters in Child Psychology was acutely aware of this occurring this summer and it greatly concerns all of us. She needs to just be a kid. Piper needs to know she is loved very much by both of us and both of our families. You telling a 6-year old that my brother Robert did "bad things" is completely inappropriate. Telling her that, "Daddy didn't show up," when we tried to coordinate with you is completely inappropriate. I tried to reschedule with you because I had a job interview; you knew this in advance. You know I offered to change dates to Monday through Monday. Then you lied and said you were leaving to Orange County. You never went to Orange County. Furthermore, you know my Mom offered to take the girls on Friday at 3:15 pm for my weeklong visitation. You declined to accept this solution. I believe you should work on being more cooperative.

Also just so you know, I go out of my way to do the opposite of PAS. I say things to the girls that are positive only. For instance, while brushing their hair, I say, "You have very pretty blonde hair like your mommy." They do not have bed wetting issues while in my care. In fact, most nights I have been waking

Sarah up to potty and I am not keeping her in pull-ups both nights. I still do the same with Piper. The girls are very good when they are with me. The only issue I have is related to Sarah talking back or not responding the first time she is asked to do something. I tend to have this resolved now by offering rewards for good, responsive behavior. However, the first few hours every time I have the girls there is a period where Piper is used to a "looser" level of discipline and she pushes the limits. Sarah simply follows suit and does whatever Piper instigates. Most of the time they play very well together, play roles of Mommy and Baby and get along well. - Seth

"Snap, fizzle, pop" and out comes the decoded email:

Tina- Having Piper in therapy concerns me because I worry about the therapist seeing the abuse that is occurring during my parenting time. If I still had legal custody, I'd definitely object to therapy. On a Father's Rights website, I discovered that abusers should beginning screaming Parental Alienation from the rooftops as a way to muddy the waters and take the spotlight off themselves. I often quiz the girls about everything going on at your house but I will be more careful now that she is in therapy. My Mom has a Master's Degree in "Sweeping Issues Under the Rug" and protecting our family image and she is acutely aware of the danger a therapist poses. Truthfully, my mom does *not* have a Master's Degree in Child Psychology but writing that makes us sound more credible just in case anyone important reads this.

Piper witnessing my brother Robert beating small puppies is a shame and could potentially affect my custody battle. I'd like to downplay that incident. In fact, I'm sure she doesn't even remember it – you are probably telling her about it every night before bed, you ALIENATOR, you! Yes, that's exactly what I'll tell the custody evaluator! Brilliant! How dare you not continue to cover for me when you sat at Starbucks waiting for 30-minutes and I was a no-show? You see, Tina, in my family, we lie for each other and to each other – you obviously weren't open to learning this during our nine years together. I had high hopes that you would learn the ropes from my mom but you failed. You little failure, you! Because I know I blew it by not showing up for a visit once again, I am going to try and cloud things by throwing in a bunch of BS and I will twist this until it looks like you are at fault. You really should learn to cooperate more with my demands and warped version of reality.

Also just so you know, I go out of my way to do the opposite of what I've read is healthy. You see, I read all of the articles that my mom sends me so that I have material for court and the evaluator but I don't give a shit about damaging the girls so I don't actually practice what I read. I often call you names like "T-Rex" to the girls and let them know that if they lived with me, we'd go to Disneyland daily and eat candy for three meals each day. Do you think that works with them? They still seem to want to go home to you at the end of visits and it's infuriating. I want nothing more in this life than for them to turn against you and live with me so I can hire a nanny to raise them. Is there a specific website where I can find nannies in short skirts? I'll ask my dad. He'll know for sure!

I have noticed the girls regressing in potty training but I would never admit this to you. Sit back and get comfortable while I explain my discipline strategies. If the girls act out, I pretend to be a big, scary bear or monster and I terrorize them until they are crying. Grabbing their wrist and squeezing super hard also works well and I've found you can also do it in public unlike hitting or slapping. When they begin screaming in pain, you just look around and roll your eyes – unsuspecting bystanders actually think they are having a temper tantrum and sympathize with me! It works wonders! Now that I have thoroughly explained my impeccable parenting techniques, I'd like to take this opportunity to slip in a jab – nothing that makes my day more than calling you a looser! Hope it stung...did it?! Please say it did!? Oh, by the way, in an effort to protect her sister, Piper assumes the role of Mommy even though that is a lot of pressure to put on a 6-year old. Someone has to protect Sarah from me and it seems Piper has taken that role in your absence. - Seth

Suggested Response:

Seth- Your attempt to portray me in a negative light is noted. I will keep you updated on suggestions from Piper's therapist.

###

Narc Decoder #17

Background: In 2010, we had our first custody evaluation which was a waste of time and money. At the time, I didn't understand NPD and the evaluator was clueless about high-conflict divorces. In 2011, Seth lost the ability to have overnight visits when he was caught lying to the judge about the whereabouts of the children. The following email was sent in 2012, almost 18-months after overnight visits were taken from him.

Original Message:

Tina- I look forward to seeing the girls on the 21st at 2:30 PM and the 22nd at 11 AM. You will recollect that the attached custody evaluation recommendation is that the girls spend three weekends with overnights with me. The other recommendation was that I could take the girls on a five-day vacation. I kindly asked you to grant a vacation to San Diego with my Mom and the girls. I do not want to have to go request a hearing with court to spend Wednesday the 1st of August through Sunday the 5th of August with the girls to bring them to San Diego Wild Animal Park and Lego Land. Would you please say this would be fine? -Seth

"Snap, fizzle, pop" and out comes the decoded email:

Tina – I love to twist reality so that it suites my personal agenda. I am hoping you will conveniently forget that I am restricted to daytime visits by reminding you of an outdated court document that is no longer relevant. I have the 2010 Custody Evaluation framed on my wall and titled, "I Fooled Her!" My family is still baffled that the court saw through me and stripped me of overnight visits. Nonetheless, my mother is here visiting and more than anything, we'd love to pretend to be a normal, healthy family and take the girls on a vacation to Southern California! Basically, it would make the perfect photo opportunity so we can snap some precious moments for court and Facebook. Take a sip of this yummy Kool-Aid and think about it for a second. You and I both know that I can't show my face in court right now so I am hoping you'll say yes. My mom loves pretending that we have a normal family and we'd appreciate you kindly driving your car off a cliff....err...no, I mean, we'd appreciate you kindly saying yes! Won't you please say "yes"?! - Seth

Suggested Response:

Seth- I intend to follow the court order exactly as it is written. We will see you at 2:30pm on the 21st and 11am on the 22nd. -Tina

###

Narc Decoder #18

Background: Because Seth stood us up for his visits so often, the Judge imposed an order that required him to notify us 24-hours in advance if he planned to exercise a visit. He often pushed boundaries and would notify me 12-hours or less in advance of his parenting time. I held firm and cancelled visits if he didn't notify us 24-hours prior to a visit. The order was a saving grace that allowed us to go on with our weekends versus being held in limbo. On one particular weekend in 2012, I emailed him to notify him that the visitation was cancelled since we hadn't heard from him.

Original Message:

Tina- I've notified you on past weekends, Wednesday and Thursday and you refused to deliver my daughters. It's not realistic to email you at 11 am on the dime, exactly 24 hours before. I drove 220 miles to get here to see my daughters. You're a vindictive, hate-filled woman who is using our daughters as pawns to get back at me. This is unacceptable and you are punishing our daughters in your pursuit to selfishly have the girls 100 percent of the time. What's it like to be full of such hatred and negative energy? It's aging your mind and outward appearance. I don't even look at your blog but I hear it's a Narcissistic statement of how great you think you are. You're a terrible mother because you keep your children from a normal, healthy relationship with their father. You are selfish, full of hate and you continuously have lied to the Commissioner verbally and in writing. Your time will come Tina for karma and justice. --Seth

"Snap, fizzle, pop" and out comes the decoded email:

Tina- I am still four hours away and had an invitation to go on a weekend pub crawl around the city. I purposely waited to email you knowing you'd cancel the visit so that I could turn this situation around and blame you. I love to say, "Deliver our daughters" because to me, they are objects and possessions. I'm a vindictive, hate-filled little boy who is causing harm to our daughters at every turn. In court, I say that I want MY daughters 100% of the time but the reality is, I will pawn them off on nannies or my mom. I'd rather pay a stranger to raise them than to pay you a penny of child support. I am full of hatred and negative energy and its aging my mind and outward appearance. I look at your blog between 10 and 100 times a day and I am consumed by the fact that you are telling the truth about me. I am also consumed with jealousy that you have a normal, healthy relationship with the girls. I am selfish, full of hate and continuously lie to the Commissioner verbally and in writing. I love making veiled threats about karma because it is too vague for you to obtain a restraining order. -Seth

Suggested Response:

Seth- I intend to follow the court order exactly as it is written. -Tina

###

Narc Decoder #19

Background: I sent childcare and medical bills to the address on file with the courts as required for two years yet he had never acknowledged them or responded. At this point, the bills that I had paid out of pocket were approaching $10,000 and that didn't include childcare for the summer. I sent Seth an email recently outlining the costs and asking for his assistance. I didn't expect his assistance however, I needed to show the courts that I attempted to communicate with him and that he is very aware of these obligations.

Original Message:

Tina- I volunteered to have time with our daughters up to two weeks every month. You refused to even let me have an exchange weekend with the girls. You further have claimed you make low

wages and work part time so you can pick the girls up from school at your leisure. Your facts remain inconsistent with someone earning income below the US poverty level. Best regards- Seth

"Snap, fizzle, pop" and out comes the decoded email:

Tina- You and I both know that having the girls for two weeks out of every month would greatly reduce the child support that I am ordered to pay each month. Since I don't pay it anyway, this is obviously a moot point. The courts revoked my overnight visits in 2011 yet I am still trying to convince them that I am qualified for 50/50 custody- as you can tell by my email. I am clearly delusional and live in a fantasy world. Since I have failed to show up for 38% of my already limited visits in 2013, we both know that I would be laughed out of court if I asked for two weeks out of every month. Currently, I can't even be depended on for five daytime visits per month!

How dare you refuse to switch weekends with me when I have parties or other social functions (i.e. drinking) on my scheduled days! Did you not get the memo that your life should revolve around mine?! I am angry that you have set boundaries and refuse to bend when I make a demand. I know how unstable I look to the courts when I can't hold a job more than 4 months at a time. Because of this, I am going to pick apart the career that you've managed to maintain and excel in during the four-year roller coaster that I've put you on. Because I am still consumed by (my lack of) money, power and prestige, I am going to attack your world which I am extremely jealous of.

Basically, I am the playground bully that never matured past the emotional age of six years old. -Seth

Suggested Response:

Document for the court. No response needed.

###

Narc Decoder #20

<u>Background</u>: Piper and Sarah have very fair skin. Seth was repeatedly bringing them home with sunburns and some of the sunburns were horrendous. On one particular occasion during our second custody evaluation, he brought the girls home with severe burns and I brought it to his attention while cc'ing the evaluator.

Original Message:

Tina- In regards to sunscreen, the girls have never been sunburnt in my attendance. I put SPF 50+ Baby Lotion on them from their faces to their toes and I spray 55+ on their scalp. They then listen to me well and wait 5 minutes before going into the water. After 4 hours I will re-apply sunscreen. I have been bringing them to the beaches and pools for 7 years, I am very concerned about protecting their fair skin. - Seth

"Snap, fizzle, pop" and out comes the decoded email:

Tina- Stop nagging! Just slather them in Aloe Vera and shut the hell up! Just drink a bottle of wine – that's what I do. It drowns out their crying and whining. I am walking a fine line here between wanting to tell you to go choke on a bottle of sunscreen and delivering my Super Dad persona to the evaluator. Pull up a seat and let me tell you a little story which allows me to put a cute, Mr. Rodger's type spin on this situation: we were at the pool and there were little fuzzy bunnies hopping all around and two doves gliding over our heads. Are you mesmerized yet? Good. I softly applied baby lotion to the girls' delicate skin and even rub it in to their cute little toes. I buy extra soft lotion with fairy sprinkles in it. I then ask them kindly to wait 5 minutes before sticking their cute bubbly toes in the water to which they reply, "Yes, Daddy!"

Okay, let's get real. I sprayed them with some sunscreen but I was in a hurry to get my margarita from the waitress so that isn't where my focus was. May or may not have remembered to put sunscreen on Sarah at all. After a few drinks, I was feeling no pain and by that time, they were already red and burnt. Oops! You do know, I've been bringing them to pools and beaches since our marriage ended because it's a great place to pick up on women and drink…err…I mean, make sandcastles with my little possessions…err….I mean, daughters. - Seth

Suggested Response:

Seth – I do not agree with your portrayal of the situation. I have attached a photo of Piper's back from the last sunburn she had while in your care and the most recent one. There are also several emails from last year in which we corresponded about the same issues. The only sunburns the girls have ever had have been while in your care. This is an ongoing issue and has been for the past few years. -Tina

Note: The *only* reason I engaged Seth to this degree was due to the custody evaluation. It was my goal to paint a clear picture for the evaluator.

Narc Decoder #21

<u>Background</u>: Shortly after the Commissioner awarded us professionally supervised visits, Seth began sending me sporadic text messages.

Original Message:

Tina- I am calling every other day to talk to my daughters as the court order states. That's my right as their father Ms. Blogger Queen. Oh, Ms. Lupus Queen as you lied to the courts about having MS. -Seth

"Snap, fizzle, pop" and out comes the decoded email:

Tina- I am mentally spiraling out of control and cannot handle the loss of power that I am currently experiencing. For this reason, I am repeatedly calling to gain a morsel of control over the three of you. I am so ANGRY that your blog has become successful and that you've continued to excel in life. I spent so many years trying to break you down- how dare you rebuild your life and your self esteem! I know that a Harvard-educated doctor and the lead neurologist at an MS facility have both diagnosed you with Multiple Sclerosis. However, I prefer the diagnosis of Lupus because while doing Google searches, I found that psychosis is a symptom of Lupus. That diagnosis allows me to project my own psychosis onto you. I continuously throw this little diagnosis into emails and text messages because I remember how upset it made you back in 2011 when I first brought it up. Obviously, that was before you understood Cluster B personality disorders. I am so frustrated that I am no longer able to get you riled up. How DARE YOU see through me and my 6-year old mind games! -Seth

Suggested Response:

None.

Narc Decoder #22

Background: I could write an entire book based on the things Seth wrote in court declarations and paperwork. When supervised visits were on the table and being considered, Seth wrote one of my favorite statements to date:

Original Statement:

Supervised visitation is not a service for men holding down such challenging careers.

"Snap, fizzle, pop" and out comes the decoding:

Supervised visitation is a service for lowlife drug addicts. I drink premium beer, wear $500 shoes, have a degree in science and a very high IQ. It is very challenging for me to hold a job for more than four months at a time due to my over-the-top ego and big mouth but nonetheless, I do not qualify for supervision due to my superiority.

Narc Decoder #23

Background: Seth was currently not exercising visits but he continued to call once per week. The phone calls were bizarre at best. He often weighed in on the girls' extracurricular activities such as telling them that he doesn't agree with horseback riding as it is "too dirty." Several months prior to the following phone call, the girls told Seth that we got a puppy. He asked what kind it was and they told him it was a black, female Standard Poodle puppy named Pixie. He laughed in his creepy, weird laugh and asked if they knew that we used to have Standard Poodles while we were married. They acknowledged that they were aware of this. Seth called back a few months later sounding completely manic. Before the girls could even say "hello," Seth blurted out, "Guess where I am?!" This was the conversation as it unfolded:

Phone Call:

"Where?" Piper asks him.

"I am buying a dog right now! Guess what kind?" Seth exclaims.

"What kind?" Piper asks him.

"A black, Standard Poodle Puppy. A little girl!" Seth proudly states in his manic voice.

The girls both stare at the phone confused.

"That's what we have," says Piper.

"What?! What did you just say? Repeat that? *YOU* have a black Standard Poodle puppy?!" he asks.

"Yes" the girls respond.

"Snap, fizzle, pop" and out comes the decoding:

Hi Girls! The Commissioner was correct: I am a complete sociopath! My goal is to cause the hairs on the back of your mom's neck to stand straight up since I know the call is on speakerphone and she can hear me. She is probably so panicked right now that she is hiding the puppy under her bed for fear I will walk past the yard and poison it. Here puppy, puppy!!! I may even file a police report stating that your mom stole my new puppy and if that doesn't work, I am going for 50/50 custody of YOUR new puppy! Brilliant! Muhahaha!

###

Narc Decoder #24

Background: Because Seth's ego could not handle supervised visits, he essentially disappeared from our lives aside from some sporadic phone calls which I was allowed to record.

After completely vanishing for 9 months, I received the following email on Piper's birthday.

Original Message:

Hi Tina- I am in town and I would really like to give the girls a hug and wish them happy birthday in person. I have gifts for them as well. Is there a time we can meet in a park for an hour or so? I know their little hearts miss their Dad. Your granting this would go a long way towards a copacetic future. – Seth

"Snap, fizzle, pop" and out comes the decoded email:

Tina- Remember me? The one who loves to ruin birthdays, holidays and special events? Thought I'd pop in on Piper and Sarah's birthday week after going MIA for almost a year to remind you all that you'll never get rid of me! I was the one who gave them their superior genes and so I'd like to celebrate my special day...oh, I mean, THEIR special day that I made possible. Did you get my name written on the birthday cake? Oh how I looove to see my name in frosting or anywhere for that matter! Just wanted to check in and see if you'd be willing to violate the court order that you fought so hard to get by allowing me to meet the girls in a park without the professional supervisor? I know their little hearts are at peace finally and I'd love to swoop in and cause chaos! Your granting my demands would go a long way towards a copacetic future in which I look forward to abusing all of you once again. -Seth

Suggested Response:

Seth- You are aware of the court order and the procedure to begin visits. I will not be violating the order but I am happy to facilitate visits once you get them started. -Tina

###

Narc Decoder #25

<u>Background</u>: It had been almost a year since Seth had seen the girls and they had been refusing his calls for quite some time.

Original Message:

Tina- I will be calling from a 610 number tonight. Please put Sarah on the phone first. You have not allowed me to talk to them since their birthdays in April. -Seth

"Snap, fizzle, pop" and out comes the decoded email:

Tina- There is no consistency on my part however, when I snap, I expect everyone to jump. What do you mean the girls don't want to talk to me anymore? Do they not know who I am? Have you not explained to them that I am a legend in my own mind? Why do they have a choice in this matter? Have them sitting and waiting for my call that may or may not come. -Seth

Suggested Response:

Seth – The girls are refusing to speak to you. This is being discussed with their therapist. -Tina

Narc Decoder #26

<u>Background</u>: Father's Day 2014. It had been a full year since Seth had seen the girls and over four months since they had accepted phone calls from him.

Original Message:

Tina- Given that it is Father's Day this weekend, I would like to see the girls at a place of your choosing for any interval of time. It's absolutely tragic that Judge Johnson and the evaluator decided it was appropriate to oust me completely from Piper and Sarah's lives because in the company of my parents on 111-degree day, I enjoyed a beer.

Every restaurant you go to, you see parents enjoying wine or beer with their children present. You know this is the case and you know you drink wine in front of the children often. It is absolutely unusual and unfair punishment not only for me but for the girls that because of this the daughters no longer can have a normal relationship or any with their father.

On another note, I work my ass off to keep my job and my career. It is incumbent upon you to tell the girls that I provide enough money to you to cover rent, food, clothing and activities for my daughters. They do not seem to be aware of this.

I used to say, back in 2010, that this divorce process has had almost no emotional effects on Piper and Sarah to people. The girls understood you had boyfriend and I was their Dad. Now it is clear by her letter, Piper in particular is going to have severe emotional scars from her loss of her father.

Tina, you grew up with a biological mother who had mental illness. Had your father not taken you to California from Illinois, she might have kidnapped you and you may not be alive had he not raised you away from your mother. What we are dealing with here is a very, very different situation. I drink high quality beer or wine as little or as much as my other friends who are parents, professionals and had working people. I do not drink every day. I exercise 2-3 hours every day sometimes 5-6 hours a day.

I am not some evil, monster as you describe me in your blog. I may have been taken by success and wanted to earn more and more money. But, that is my personality, to try to be the best in my field. It is time that you turn the mirror on you and realize that the damage this divorce has caused me has now been magnified on our daughters.

I disagree completely with the Judge's punitive measures against me. I could understand if I smoked pot or did drugs to require supervised visits but he clearly hates me and you know this. Thus, you dragged me in front of him 30 times until he snapped on me permanently. He was sick and tired of seeing us and I do not blame him. This was all you. You constantly harassed me with court hearings in the middle of my work week. You cost me jobs because of this Tina. All I wanted was to spend one week a month with Piper and Sarah. The custody evaluation buried me. Now, the daughters are in emotional turmoil.

I would really like to see the girls please. Even if we see them at the Children's Museum and you're there. I don't really care. I just want to see them. Thank you for your consideration. -Seth

"Snap, fizzle, pop" and out comes the decoded email:

Tina- Given that it is Father's Day, I feel entitled to see MY daughters. MY possessions. You know, the ones that I haven't seen in a year? Seeing them on Father's Day would certainly boost my ego and I would be able to report back to my mommy that I am a good son who cares so much about my children. Using phrases like "intervals of time" makes me feel important. Do I sound important to you?

I think it's completely tragic that the court saw through me. How dare they have an issue with the fact that I, as a severe alcoholic, drank alcohol against court orders in a bar with MY possessions present? Ignore the fact that I drove them after drinking. It's tragic that I was held accountable. It was premium beer for God's sake. I should receive some slack for the fact that I don't drink the same beer that lower life forms consume. It was PREMIUM beer, Tina. Can you grab me a beer while I sit here and project my alcohol issues on you? I know you drink wine and I don't think it's fair that you don't have DUIs, Drunk in Publics and Wet 'n Reckless charges on your record. You probably do...you probably slept with the police officers to get away with it all! Damn you!

I am going to ignore the fact that in addition to the violation of court orders, there was a 43-page report that could make Cyndi Lauper burst into song... "I see your true colors shining through." Can you please make the girls aware of the child support that I pay? Have them send me a thank you card in the morning because they would not be able to enjoy cereal if it weren't for me. You are all so ungrateful. Everything you have is technically mine. Did you know that? You should send me a thank you card also.

Regarding the letter that Piper wrote. First of all, I'm sure this was a coached letter. Since when has she been allowed to set boundaries and express feelings? That's just weird. Make her stop immediately. This is the part where I remind you of your dysfunctional childhood. I do this in an effort to make you feel bad and in turn, make myself feel better. Do you feel bad? Is it working? Did I mention that I drink high-quality beer? I do, so there!

I am the evil monster that you portray me to be in your blog. How dare you tell the truth about me? It literally eats me alive. Can you please turn the mirror on yourself and realize what you have done? Enough already! Give me the mirror back so I can see myself again! Damn! I'm hot!

I disagree with the measures the court took to hold me accountable for my behavior. How dare they do this to me! I don't do drugs. I drink premium beer. I am not a loser. My mom said I was perfect. This was all your fault for telling them the truth about me. I believe the distorted version of reality that I have spun in my head and so should you. So should the courts. You constantly held me accountable for my behavior. How dare you!

Now that I am finished telling you what a cold, evil person you are, can we just put this all behind us and forget the past five years? I'd love for you to violate court orders this weekend by bringing the girls to the museum so that I can pretend to be a dad on Father's Day. Can you dress them in a color that compliments my blue shirt? I need a new photo for Facebook. Sound good to you? Thank you for your consideration. – Seth

Suggested Response:

Seth- Visits with the girls are to be professionally supervised. Please refer to the court orders dated July 10, 2013 for instructions on how to visit the girls. If you are confused, your attorney can surely explain the orders to you. – Tina

###

Narc Decoder #27

Background: Seth had been absent from the girls' lives for over a full year. Six months prior to the following email, the girls began refusing his calls. He then resorted to sending text messages to Piper's phone which was a direct violation of our court order. I sent him an email with a screen print of the message letting him know that I would be discussing the issue with her therapist and requesting that he stop sending text messages.

Original Message:

Tina- I am going to call my daughters and leave messages every week. Why are you not letting me talk to Sarah if Piper feels abandoned by me? The last time you let me talk with my daughters was on April 19th and April 22nd. You didn't even take my calls on Father's Day!!! I did not abandon my daughters. I plan to be very involved in their lives when they can think for themselves. I have had to take on the mentality that a soldier would take if he or she were headed off to war overseas and couldn't see their family. I am 100% confident they will understand when they're older everything I have tried to do since 2009 to be involved as much as possible while getting back on my feet financially. I would still drive 440 miles every weekend as I was doing in 2009 to see my daughters if the court had not cancelled my visits, eliminated my expendable income which you get and been fair in this process.

Why don't you tell Piper that I pay for all of her health insurance, the roof over her head and all of her food working very hard covering the entire state of California as an Account Manager in the very stressful and competitive sales environment? If you want to reverse the damage, why don't you agree to drop child support in half? I can then afford to rent a car and rent a hotel room and pay a supervisor to see them? You have no idea what it is like for me to not get to see my daughters on their birthdays or on Father's Day. Every time I see a father with their young children it breaks my heart. Every night I go to sleep and every morning I wake up I feel a deep pain in my soul missing them.

Irrespective your constant process of Parental Alienation Syndrome has taken full form and is now causing our daughters severe emotional scars. I believe 100% that you have purposely encouraged Piper's adverse feelings towards me. Even your act of bringing the girls to counselors to extract any negative things you could use in court the day after visits is so obviously a tactic of PAS. I am blown away to this day that the evaluator and Judge did not see right through you. Furthermore, right from the beginning of the requirement for supervised visits you arbitrarily cancelled the court order and stopped taking my calls every other day. You just decided on your own that I only get to call them once a week.

All that being said, I am sick and tired of your slander and defamation around the community of me, my father, my mother and my brother. People all over town came up to me constantly and asked me if it knew about the blog you were writing. You really should be ashamed of yourself. You have emotionally and permanently scarred our daughters. All you had to do back in 2009 was let me see my daughters every other weekend and none of this would be occurring. The court in my opinion acted in a way that is excessively punitive to me and my daughters. I am tired of the constant stress of going to court 220 miles from where I must live. I am tired of Judge Johnson's heavy-handedness towards me when you have lied about having multiple sclerosis, lied about the incident (that did not occur) at church... it goes on and on. The Judge never punished you for lying in court documents and verbally under oath. You literally lied under oath in written documents and on court transcript. If I had enough money to pay another $5,000 to attorneys, I would prove it. Ultimately, I am just over the whole process. I hope the girls

*will understand in their teenage years I put the best effort in I
possibly could. -Seth*

"Snap, fizzle, pop" and out comes the decoded email:

Tina- I don't give a shit about what is best for MY daughters. I
don't care what they want. I never have. I plan to call and leave
messages every week because I refuse to let you and MY
daughters have peace. I last spoke to them on their birthdays
and I am pissed that they didn't send me a gift and a thank you
card. They wouldn't have life if it weren't for me – I deserve a
gift. The girls even refused my calls on Father's Day!!! I sat
home drinking all day and lied to my friends about having
plans with my daughters. Sometimes, I even pretend to talk to
them on the phone when I am on dates. Women think it's SO
cute!

Oh, by the way, I did abandon my daughters because my ego
couldn't handle the rejection or the thought of a professional
supervisor monitoring my every slimy move. When the girls
turn 18 and we are out of the prying eyes of the court minions,
I plan to sell them on my victim story. Until then, I have to
take on the mentality of a severe alcoholic to drown out my
sorrows and blur out the inner turmoil that eats at me night
and day. I am obsessed with winning and control. Having the
court see through me was a huge loss in my mind. I am 100%
confident the girls will believe my lies when they're older. I'm
very convincing. If the courts had not cancelled my visits, your
lives would still revolve around me standing you up, calling
drunk and abusing the children.

111

Any therapist that I paid off would support my request for you to tell Piper, an 8-year old, that I pay for all of her health insurance, the roof over her head and her food. Totally healthy to talk to children about adult matters. Probably best not to mention that I am $46,000 in arrears. Details, details. MY daughter is so ungrateful and that's your fault also. I'm sure it's from your side of the gene pool. By the way, you still haven't thanked me for the 10 years of abuse you endured. Like mother, like daughter. If you want to help contribute to my beer and travel fund, why don't you agree to drop child support in half? You have no idea what a hit my ego took when I read the evaluator's report. I am so good at convincing people that I am super dad – still not sure why it didn't work on this round. Every time I see a father with their young children, the empty dark spot where most people have a heart gets a weird crampy feeling because I can no longer post current photos on social media. Puppies and children get so many more likes than the selfies I take. That's actually a great idea. I am brilliant! I should get a puppy! I wonder if you can rent them by the hour?

Irrespective (big word, right?! I do have a really high IQ) of your refusal to cover for me and lie as my mother would have done for my father, our daughters will have severe emotional scars due to my actions but like with anything, I will turn it around on you. PAS is commonly thrown out by abusers in an effort to muddy the water. Is it muddy yet? I can't see you! How dare Piper have adverse feelings towards me! Kids should be seen and not heard. Those damn counselors really exposed me. I can't believe they weren't impressed by all of the photos from Disneyland. Do you realize how much of my beer money I spent that day? I drink premium beer and it's pricey. I am blown away to this day that the evaluator and Judge saw through me. How dare they not believe that you were a crack-smoking, alcoholic.

This is a small town and I am sick of you telling the truth about my family. My mom has busted her ass my entire life to hide my father's indiscretions and to burn our family's dirty laundry. People all over town are ignoring me or making comments about your blog. You have permanently scarred my family name. All you had to do back in 2009 was let me abuse my daughters every other weekend and none of this would be occurring. The court in my opinion was very mean to me and that's not nice! I am tired of the constant stress of going to court 220 miles from my favorite bars. I am tired of Judge Johnson's heavy-handedness towards me. I constantly lied in court documents and verbally under oath. If I had enough money, I'd drink extra premium in bars. I did research on TMZ and I drink the same beer that Kanye West drinks. Bam! Ultimately, I am just over this whole process. -Seth

Suggested Response:

None.

Narc Decoder #28

Background: Seth was repeatedly calling the girls and they were refusing his calls. I leaned heavily on their therapist for direction and she supported their decision to end contact.

Original Message:

Tina- You've blocked me from contact with my daughters. I can't text them. You won't let me talk to them. I don't have enough money left after all you get in child support to travel, pay for overnights and pay a third party. How about I go to counseling with them? This is tragic for their little minds and hearts. Research what you've done: Parental Alienation Syndrome. It's clear and evident from everyone I have discussed this with. You think it's healthy for Piper and Sarah to be cut off from their dad? If you care, share this video with them, Tina. This is the last weekend they saw me. I guarantee you they miss me all the time. You can still reverse the damage you have done. -Seth

"Snap, fizzle, pop" and out comes the decoded email:

Tina- I have chosen to blow my $7,000 per month salary on bars and alcohol versus spending money to rent a car and hire a supervisor to visit the girls. You are probably wondering why I don't have a car any longer. It got repossessed because I refuse to live within my means. You have to understand how difficult it is to impress the ladies without a car.

I am hoping that you will forget that huge episode last year when I wanted to meet with Piper and her therapist — I know that Piper doesn't want me to attend therapy with her but since when have I ever cared what the girls want? Oh and by the way, I've recently started diagnosing by Wikipedia and according to my thorough research, you have a disorder that causes you to protect our children from abuse. Damn you.

Do you think it's really healthy for the girls to live a peaceful, normal childhood far away from my superior genes and influence? Without me in their lives, they are going to grow up to be below average just like you. Please share this video with them. This video is the last weekend that I spent with them. To refresh your memory, this is the weekend that I took them to a bar and drank alcohol against court orders. After that fun little episode, I put them in the car and drove them with alcohol in my system because I am really that arrogant and as we all know, court orders do not apply to me. Court orders are for regular members of society – not men like *me*. This was also the weekend my parents were visiting. In this video, you will see my stellar performance that I refer to as, "Tales of Super Dad." I was putting on my best performance in this particular episode because my mom, Cleo, was filming and I'm still trying to convince her that I am normal. She captured my normalcy on tape! Further proof that you are lying about me! Ha!

I guarantee that the girls miss me. How could they not?! I mean, after all….I lie to them, physically hurt them, emotionally abuse them. What is NOT to miss with this stellar McDaddy package? You can reverse the damage that you've done (to ME) by letting bygones be bygones and just forgetting about the past five years. You've always been one to hold grudges…very sad and pathetic if you ask me. -Seth

Suggested Response:

Seth- Please contact the court appointed supervisor to begin visits. -Tina

###

Narc Decoder #29

Background: After 15 months, Seth finally began the process to start supervised visits. True to Narcissistic fashion, he wanted to schedule the very first visit on my 40th birthday. It would have almost been laughable except for the fact that he was about to turn the girls' lives upside down once again. Initially, he was trying to use a supervisor that wasn't court approved. I reminded him of the court ordered supervisors, contacted the girls' therapist and suggested reunification therapy to start with.

Original Message:

Tina- The recommendation was for Nuevo Supervision Services and they never returned my emails and the voicemail doesn't accept messages for over a year. I called her multiple times last year when this first started and received no reply. I have been trying ever since April. I finally looked up the National Registry of approved Supervisors and Elena is an approved supervisor. There is no way I will go to someone you have a previous relationship with as you did with the woman from the Women's Shelter with whom you feigned an abuse issue 4+ years ago to gain her favor. I don't see anywhere where the person you are stating is recommended.

Furthermore, the damage you have caused by using our divorce and the court system to profit from not one but two books now is unconscionable. I purposely removed myself from all of your world because I know you were using the court system to get chapters for your first book. Using child support money to follow me around with private investigators and going to the extreme of hiring young girls to follow me around where I live is disturbing and is considered stalking. I believe that you are not using the child support money in the proper manner to provide and care for the girls but rather pay private investigators to follow me when I am on my own time. Why are you still so obsessed with me 5 years after I divorced you? Let me live my own life and move on.
-Seth

"Snap, fizzle, pop" and out comes the decoded email:

Tina- It's been a full year since I've seen the girls and in that time, I've accidentally drunk-dialed the supervision service multiple times. However, I have never once attempted to contact them while sober. Recently, my mom came to visit for the summer and put pressure on me to impress the family with my superb parenting skills. To make my mom happy, I have finally decided to reach out and touch someone. You know, those people who were appointed to supervise me.

Have I mentioned that my ego can't handle the thought of supervision but I am willing to do anything to please my mom? I probably won't really follow through — I will take the first steps and then tell her how mean you are and that you are preventing me from seeing my possessions…errrr….I mean, MY daughters. I wrote in the email that I have been trying to contact the company since April but you and I both know that's B.S. I just like writing things like that in case the court gets a wild hair and decides to believe anything I say! It's worth a shot, right? Right? You know I'm right…I'm always right!

Elena is an approved supervisor and since I spoke with her first, I am confident that I can sell her on how evil you are…and how I've been wronged. There is no way I will go to someone who could have potentially read our court file. You know how much I hate being exposed. I don't see anywhere in the court docs that says the person you are suggested is recommended (I'm covering my eyes, haha!) because am choosing to twist reality to suite my agenda and needs. That shouldn't be news to you - I love twisting reality!

Furthermore ("Furthermore" is one of my favorite words because it makes me sound in control and smart), the damage you have caused by telling the truth about our divorce to profit from not one but two books now is unconscionable (I should probably get a thesaurus since I use "unconscionable" in every email). I purposely removed myself from your world because the Commissioner and Evaluator saw through me and I could not handle it. Damn you for telling people the truth again!

I hate the fact that you can survive financially without me. It goes against everything I've ever told you and pisses me off. I know that I recently got fired from yet another job and no longer pay child support. I know that my arrears is over $40,000 and I hate that you have become self-sufficient. I hate it. I hate it! I remember back in the good old days when my frequent terminations would make you cry and scramble to figure out how to buy groceries. Gosh, I sure miss those days!

It infuriates me that you've used a private investigator to show my true colors. Being followed has made me so incredibly paranoid that I now think young girls are following me. They are everywhere! Blondes, brunettes, red heads! I also believe that you are not using the child support money that I no longer pay you to properly care for the girls. I firmly believe that you are obsessed with me — you are, aren't you? Everyone else is....you are, right?! Let me live my own life, free of rules and court orders and we'll all be happy. PS. Isn't it ironic that I spent so many years correcting your grammar and mine is horrendous? Let me figure out a way to blame you for my grammatical errors and I will get back to you. I'm sure your stupidity rubbed off on me during our marriage. -Seth

Suggested Response:

Seth- As the order states, you are to call Nuevo Supervision Services or Jane Smith. I have been in contact with both and will wait for confirmation. -Tina

###

CHAPTER 6

MESSAGES FROM THE BATTLEFIELD

The Narc Decoder has become a way for those in the trenches to find humor, comradery and a light at the end of the tunnel. I am happy to share some of these messages straight off the battlefield from the men and women who inspire me to keep speaking out and educating the masses on Narcissistic Personality Disorder. I am so thankful that these men and women trusted me with the intimate details of their custody battle and to protect their identity, all names and locations have been changed. For your viewing pleasure, we kept the poor grammatical structure of the original messages intact for authenticity.

Narc Decoder Sample #1

Original Message:

Amber: I will be in Houston until Wednesday night. The girls want me to pick them up at 10:30 on Thanksgiving. Bob Anderson passed away last week and they are just now planning a memorial service. I will try to go to Florida if they hold services until after Thanksgiving. – Matt

Amber: Matt- I'm so sorry to hear that! Do you know what he died of?

Matt: I don't know. Kurt and I think he must have died at home alone because his passing was only discovered by friends yesterday. If he was with family or in the hospital, we would have known. He traveled all summer. He was very concerned and sad about our divorce. Kurt just saw him in September and he was fine.

"Snap, fizzle, pop" and out comes the decoded email:

You killed Bob.

###

Narc Decoder Sample #2

Original Message:

Kathy- Hudson's day to day behavior has continued to be a major concern to me. For instance, I have attached his current daily communicator which just encompasses the first three days of the week which includes: hitting someone, calling someone a, "meanie," arguing during math stations, not following directions and disrupting the class during instruction. This is highly concerning to me and I feel like I am in somewhat of a tough position to help given my significantly reduced possession of the boys. Hopefully this is not a trend. I will do what I can. I believe Hudson is capable of better behavior than he is currently exhibiting. -Jay

"Snap, fizzle, pop" and out comes the decoded email:

Kathy- I have to act like I'm a good father, so here goes. I plan to use lots of big words and long run-on sentences to make myself sound smart and important because I am both of those things. This week, our son cried out for help and it is all your fault. I will ignore the fact that you have been begging for over a year for us to be on the same page when it comes to parenting and discipline. Certainly his behavior has nothing to do with the fact that I have been beating my new wife for over a year, culminating in loss of 50/50 custody while I face felony assault charges. Hudson hitting friends can't have anything to do with the fact that he saw me beat my wife. Nah, no way.

I love any excuse to bother you and blame you. Poor me. I can't do anything because you have been such a jerk and have taken away my time. It wasn't the near death beating I gave my wife....no. It's because you are bitter and high conflict. I have zero respect for you. -Jay

Narc Decoder Sample #3

Original Message:

Elaine- As you know today and this weekend is my parenting time with the children. You have coached them through this whole process of divorce and the fact is, you have poisoned them against me week after week. You've manipulated the counselor into saying that my nephew, Tom, is a danger to the children which is a lie and you know it. I'm not going to see Tara today but I'm not giving up on my children. I would never turn the kids against you because just like the Judge said, the children need both a mother and a father. You have taken one child from me already- this is violation. -Ernie

"Snap, fizzle, pop" and out comes the decoded email:

Elaine- One thing is for sure, I am hysterically lonely and my bizarre, dysfunctional nephew, Tom, is NOT a sufficient source of supply! I am completely lost without you around to remind me to shower and brush my teeth. Can you remind me again when my parenting time is? Nevermind, instead, let me indulge you with ludicrous accusations. I've been silent lately because I am still fantasizing about being married to you and the massive amounts of attention you gave me. I thought for sure since the new counselor is a female, she would be easier to manipulate with all of my charm and lies than our last male counselor. When Roy harms the children, he will take the blame and *not* me so your idea that the kids are in danger is irrelevant. Stop being so focused on the arrest warrant that he has out for him right now. Details, details. If I didn't have Roy's full support, I could not keep up this exhausting charade and failure is not an option here. I'm going to WIN! If you are going to keep exposing the truth about me, I will continue to use the Judge's theory to get my way and turn the kids against you. -Ernie

###

Narc Decoder Sample #4

Original Message:

Anna - I wish I had a mirror to have you see how you come across in your presentation. Maybe there would be a slim possibility you could see how angry, inflexible, demanding a person that you are. Why would anybody want to work anything out with you! You do not know the first thing about being

accommodating, understanding, or professional for any matters. So you run to your attorney to find solutions. Besides, the selfishness that is your true self. All you know to do is fight, fight, fight. How very sad because one day it will have an effect on your existence if you keep it up. Find a better way to channel your anger that life is not fair for you or you may face the consequences. Soon there will be no need to consider "the Family Wizard" for communication because I will rarely have any contact with you except to discuss logistics. So it is totally off the table. Period.

I, too, have plans for myself and our daughters, so you are not privileged in setting what weekend day we do the exchange. In fact, as I said before, I gave you 18 months of many episodes of flexibility and that will not be easy to get anymore. You cannot make Sundays a unilateral condition for hours that were decided by my employer, speaking of being unilateral. Life does not care what you think! I will not waste anymore of my valuable time today with your expressions of whining and discontent.

"Snap, fizzle, pop" and out comes the de-coded email:

Anna- I wish I had a mirror right now so that I could see myself. I could spend hours staring into my own eyes. Have I told you lately how angry I am at my loss of power since our marriage ended? Yes, I'm angry, inflexible and demanding, and all of those feelings have escalated tremendously since I can no longer control you. Damn you. I refuse to compromise or work anything out with you – it's my way or the highway. Didn't you read the fine print on the pre-nup? I do not know the first thing about being accommodating, understanding or professional but instead of taking ownership for my own shortcomings; I am going to project my faults on to you. Heck, it's always worked in the past.

I hate that you have an attorney to turn to for advice – why can't you just let me continue to control and manipulate you?! It's quite infuriating. I love to fight, fight, fight. This constant drama feeds me because I know that it affects you. I LOVE to affect you. Speaking of love, did you know that I am actually incapable of that? Thank God I am so manipulative because that's how I am able to fool women just like I fooled you. Have you seen my mirror lately? Aren't you supposed to keep track of my things?

Our Family Wizard? Are you joking? Do you really think that I want my words and actions to be monitored? Ha! I want access to you by all means possible – text, phone, email, in person and while shouting from the rooftops. You want ME to agree to something that YOU think is a good idea? Ha! Did I mention that I am a control freak and a program like that would not work well for me? The only way that I will agree to use that program is if it somehow becomes my idea. I will be sure to request that YOU be required to use it while we are in front of the Judge because doing so will play into my claim that you are harassing me and suggest the program will put an end to your persistent abuse. By the way, have you ever heard of a program called, "Our Family Wizard?" I happened to find it online yesterday and I think we should begin to use it. I am tired of the constant harassment from you.

You want me to be flexible on times for visitation. I'm sorry but that is a one-way street. You must adhere to the court order word for word, however, I will let you know when I need you to bend. Oh, by the way, next weekend doesn't work well for me as I have a lunch date. I'll need you to take our daughters for a few extra hours.

Have I mentioned how valuable my time is? I should get paid to just be awake and breathing. Now that I've thoroughly fed my sick, deranged ego, I am going to sit here and gloat knowing that you are on the receiving end of my latest attack. I'm going to envision you breaking down crying because that is like a high to me.

Suggested response:

I plan to adhere to the visitation schedule as it is written. Thank you, Anna.

Note: Nothing more. Nothing less. Polite and business-like. In a healthy co-parenting relationship, there is give and take. Flexibility is something offered by both parents. Unfortunately, it is a one-way street when you are dealing with a Narcissist. Always adhere to the schedule as it is written. A simple request opens you up for an attack such as the one above. With a Narcissist, it is imperative that you do not deviate from the court order.

###

Narc Decoder Sample #5

Original Message:

Robyn- I think it would be good for our children if you and I could exchange, at least, some token greetings when we cross paths. I understand that you and your parents are still generating quite a bit of hostile emotions, however it would really be best if these were not displayed in front of the boys. I'm sure you are trying to make some type of statement with your eagerness to usher me outside and shutting the door in my face without even a "Hello," but all you are demonstrating is that it's ok to be disrespectful to others, including one's own family. As this is something we both seem to be grappling with from the boys, perhaps we can reevaluate our own behavior and try to set a better example for our children. -Tom

"Snap, fizzle, pop" and out comes the decoded email:

Robyn- I know that I am guilty of infidelity, monetary fraud, deceit and seem to be practicing laughable self-aggrandizement on a regular basis but I ask that you put that all aside for the time being and give me a big hug and maybe even a peck on the cheek when you see me. When I violate your boundaries by entering your home, how dare you usher me out without letting me give you a slap on the ass for old time's sake. I'd like for you to reevaluate your behavior because it's hurting my ego. -Tom

###

Narc Decoder Sample #6

Original Message:

Leandra- I'm on the fence about Christmas. The kids will either have Santa gifts or notes in their stockings saying to work on better behavior, listening and respecting their parents. When I mentioned that "Santa is watching," they don't even seem phased. -Chuck

"Snap, fizzle, pop" and out comes the decoded email:

Leandra- I'm in a bit of a panic. You see, I spent money on a snowboarding trip this week even though I am playing the poverty card. You know how I love snow bunnies! Now my money is completely gone and I'm not sure what to do. Besides, when we get to my apartment on Christmas Eve, I won't have an audience of family members so I don't think it's worth the effort to have Santa show up this year. This also gives me an opportunity to teach the kids to respect me more regardless of what a jerk I am to them. -Chuck

###

Narc Decoder Sample #7

Original Message:

<u>Sheena</u>: Asking me to do homework with Amanda (second grade) on my Tuesday nights is totally unreasonable! -Steve

<u>Sheena</u>: Most parents enjoy doing homework with their children. You believe this is unreasonable?

<u>Steve</u>: To ask me to do homework during the four hours I see her on Tuesday is beyond unreasonable. The fact that you can't

see that is unshockingly sad. I will enjoy my parenting time despite your attempt to control and interrupt it.

"Snap, fizzle, pop" and out comes the decoded email:

Sheena- The children are MY possessions and this is MY time. No one will control ME. I have no desire to be a real parent. I prefer to play the Disneyland parent role. Please let me know when report cards come out so I can take full credit for their good grades. Do you really want me helping with homework considering the fact that I believe "unshockingly" is a word? - Steve

###

Narc Decoder Sample #8

Original Message:

Shauna- I would like to pick the boys up on Wednesday as close to 5:30 as possible. I have a parent/teacher conference at OMS at 6:00 and I want to make sure I'm there on time. I'm unable to open the receipt for urgent care. What is it for and please tell me: why am I just now finding out that there was a trip to urgent care? -Jon

Shauna's Response: Jon- Yes, you can pick them up at 5:30pm on Wednesday, January 15th. I have re-saved and re-attached the receipt from Urgent Care in the amount of $20.42 dated 12/20/13. The visit date was 12/7/2013. This was the time you took Andy to Urgent Care for pink eye. -Shauna

"Snap, fizzle, pop" and out comes the decoded email:

Shauna- you are responsible for my memory. I hope to remember that. Can you remind me? You are also my secretary and should remain on guard because I will jump at the opportunity showcase you as a bad co-parent, taking the children to medical appointments and not informing me. -Jon

Narc Decoder Sample #9

Original Message:

Melanie- I don't really know how we've gotten to this point. I know I have been far from perfect in our marriage but I am not this terrible person you must think I am. Just a week and a half ago we were talking about having another child and now here we are on the verge of divorce. I don't believe that's what you want. I am never going to be perfect or not make mistakes but I was advised when I was thinking of leaving that I needed to stay and try to make it work for the kids. I chose to stay and try which is what you wanted. I will never be perfect but I will continue to try if for no other reason for the sake of my kids. If you think you and I need to be apart that's fine, I completely understand but I would ask that you at least let me spend good quality time with my children. You must have been in love with me at some point so I must not be all bad. I ask you to consider that now. Even if there's nothing to work out between you and I and we go our separate ways forever the kids still need a father and while you might marry someone else I will always be their dad. I want to be a part of my kid's lives. There are millions of women out there who want that but can't get it. If you think about it I am not really asking for much from you just to be with my kids. Think about it and let me know when you want to come and sort through our stuff with me and I will help. -Thomas

"Snap, fizzle, pop" and out comes the decoded email:

My Property- I refuse to let anyone see how Narcissistic I am, so I am going to write this email in an effort to create a paper trail showing that all I want is time with my kids. I'm really not THAT bad. You have to be unbalanced because you went from wanting a baby to wanting a divorce. You couldn't really know your own mind because you aren't that smart. I put up with you for the sake of the kids and now you want to leave? I am never going to change, so if you want to leave go ahead, but I am not leaving MY home. All I want is time with MY kids and you need to stop trying to protect them. If I'm all that bad and you fell in love with me what does that say about you? The kids belong to me, and you can't take what is mine. Once again, I need to remind you that lots of woman would *kill* for a man like me, so something must be wrong with you. If you want to come over and try to take your stuff while I stand over you in an attempt to intimidate you while telling you what you can and can't have, I will allow it and actually derive my Narcissistic feed from the control I have. -Your Master

Suggested Response:

None. In this particular email, there isn't anything involving the children that needs responding to. Any attempt at engaging will only feed him and encourage him to continue.

Narc Decoder Sample #10

Original Message:

Martha- When I picked Savanna up today from school, she had a scab on her face and she was complaining of her stomach hurting. She then showed me that she had another scab on her stomach that came from her "falling out of a tree while mommy was grading homework." She went on to explain that you were with Sophia's brother and sister grading homework and you were inside, not outside with her. I appreciate that her recollection of what may have happened may not be 100% accurate so I'm not accusing you of anything rather bringing this to your attention.

However, if babysitting is interfering with your ability to juggle 5 kids at the same time (3 kids you're watching, Stephie and Savanna), let me know and I'll take Savanna while you're working and return her when you're off. Savanna falling out of trees and showing up with scabs on her face and stomach would be something better communicated prior to an exchange and appreciated greatly. Thank you -Richard

"Snap, fizzle, pop" and out comes the decoded email:

Martha- I know that it's completely normal for a child to have scabs and stomach aches but I wanted to let you know that it's your fault that our daughter had a scab and a stomach ache. This email is intended to show everyone that: a) I'm an amazing, caring dad b) to make sure that I rub into your face that you are a bad mom and you don't know how to take care of children! So here I go!!! Seatbelt fastened?

You should know that in another reality, the one that I created, you have homework and you do this "homework" inside while leaving a 3-year old and the other children that you watch outside all by themselves. While alone outside, they are all on a tree ...really, really high up. They just dangle there for hours on end. Unattended. This is another great opportunity to let you know that even though you are available and capable of caring for our daughter, I will try to take her away from you because I know it will destroy you and that's my goal. Destroying you will make my really sad, pathetic and empty life happier. Really going out on a limb here (get it…the kids…in a tree) and believing that I, being a superior being, am a better parent then you. I know that the court will believe everything I say because I am truly special and unique.

Now here is where I want to have a chance to include that not only you are neglectful and careless but also this is a wonderful time to bring up that you aren't competent to watch the four children that you been successfully caring for over the past year. I'd like you to ignore the fact that I have returned our daughter with 2nd degree burns and bruises on her legs in shape of my finger prints and focus on a tummy ache and scratch. I'm not really thankful, I'm just writing "thanks" for the judge to see that I am extremely polite. -Richard

Narc Decoder Sample #11

<u>Background</u>: Stacy emailed him on Tuesday about Termanix coming to the house between 8am and 10am on Friday. He does not work during the day.

Original Message:

Stacy- I realize I probably should've replied to your query sooner, but I'd appreciate more advance notice of all scheduling needs in the future. I find it hard to believe you only found out about this on Tuesday afternoon. Also, I'm tired of you making appointments that require my attendance and/or assistance without me actually being a part of the appointment making process. Please provide options for me the next time you make an appointment that requires my help. This includes but is not limited to teachers, plumbers, exterminators, therapists and hair stylists. I'll stay home for this appointment because I didn't let you know sooner, but I am not staying home for any more appointments that I had no part in making as we move forward. -Keith

"Snap, fizzle, pop" and out comes the decoded email:

Stacy- I know I can't keep up with dates and appointments no matter how many advance notices and reminders you spoon-feed me. Just like yesterday when I failed to show up for a parent appointment with Devin's therapist even though you emailed me about it 10 days prior and sent me a text the morning of. You see, I generally don't read your messages because ultimately you will be to blame for every mistake I make anyway. That being said, I don't like having to sacrifice any of my abundant free time to do a favor for anyone, especially you. I'm sad that you don't give me any attention so I'm asking that you go out of your way to include me in small decisions like appointment making so I can then give you the run around by not responding or making something very simple into something difficult. I will stay home for your Terminex appointment because I would probably be sitting on the couch in my underwear anyway. However, going forward I will not agree to help you in any way because I want you to suffer for not kissing my butt!! -Keith

Suggested Response:

"Thank you."

###

Narc Decoder Sample #12

Original Message:

Joan- I wanted to share something with you. This is what I posted on my Facebook page tonight. "I remember my ex telling me that when I was deployed, my youngest, Anna, then age 6, wanted to pray for me. Love you, Anna. Daddy made it home safe. Changed, as we all are, but safe. And to my ex, thank you for being there for our children. I cannot fathom the stress that you endured. God bless. -Anty

"Snap, fizzle, pop" and out comes the decoded email:

Joan- I am stating that I posted this on Facebook but I am just trying to engage you. The reality is, I do not have any friends but follow our daughter's high school girl friends on there. Creepy, I know. I am secretly hoping you will waste your time trying to find my profile.

It is Veteran's Day and I was just sitting here reminiscing about how good I had it when I was married to you. As you know, I do not believe in God. I believe I *am* God so there can be no one else that is God. I am a self-proclaimed Buddhist and have converted my oldest daughter to Buddhism. I know you and Anna believe in God and pray to God but I'm confused. Are you praying to me or are you confused? Anna was six years old when I went to the Middle East for a year. I was stationed in an air conditioned palace the whole year and did not see combat but I love making others think that I was on the front lines. I wish that my military friends would have kept their mouths shut and not told you the truth about my time overseas. I know Anna wishes now that I had not come back but I will never admit that. I don't know why everyone gets so upset when I have her sleep with me or model her new bikini for me. I know you always have been and always will be there for the children because you care more about them than you do yourself. I cannot fathom that. Seems really bizarre and selfless. Maybe you should speak to a therapist and start to prioritize. In my world, it's all about me all the time. I say God Bless only because I think I am God. - Signing off as, "Anty" versus Anthony because I am intoxicated once again.

Suggested Response:

None.

###

Narc Decoder Sample #13

Original Message:

Lisa- You screwed up, just own it and move on. 48-years old, three therapists, a failed marriage and hundreds of thousands of dollars in attorney's fees and you still haven't learned the value of this very simple behavior. -John

"Snap, fizzle, pop" and out comes the decoded email:

Lisa- I am an angry 50-year old man. Why am I angry? Because I wasn't allowed to do whatever I wanted while married and then, you have the audacity to divorce me. Because you left me, YOU tarnished my image with my parents, my family and the community. -John

Suggested Response:

None.

###

Narc Decoder Sample #14

Original Message:

Susan- I think the best thing would be for you to give us full custody. When I ask for an update and you say fine but in reality he threw up and had diarrhea in the morning and you

still take to school. WTF is wrong with you. Yes the day after he was in the ER all day as well. You don't do what was required for him with the poop sample in two days. I have zero respect for you none. Not that you care cause you don't care about the kids. I can go on and on. When I dropped Kenny off Wednesday after the ER Noelia is outside in short sleeves playing when it was cold enough for a coat. I have asked before for full custody and we think we may need to try and get this now. You send lies on simple questions about the kids health. I don't plan to send shit to you anymore. You want it to go to court since what you send me is BS. This pisses me off beyond belief that someone would do this when it comes to the kids. No way in hell he should have been at school Thursday. We also in the past have told you anytime we can take them. Also you told Kenny that we didn't tell you about the location of the hospital. Yes he saw the emails and knows that story is BS. Be ready we plan to file for full custody. Why would you say fine when he puked and had diarrhea? Cause you didn't want to take off work? Why would you tell me fine. Last time I checked puking and diarrhea even a little is not fine? What world do you live in? The kids best interest is what we want. There is a huge list or questionable things we have documented and this maybe the last straw. -Billy

"Snap, fizzle, pop" and out comes the decoded email:

Susan- I can't stand that you are a great mom and I feel threatened that you just bought a house. In an effort to rain on your excitement, I want to stomp my proverbial feet and pout like a child. I will now insult you with my standard line of crap to try and rattle your feathers because I once saw how it tears you apart. I know it's been since 2009 that this process began, but I just can't ever give up my fight and my rage is pointed to you, so here it comes. I have no clue how to take care of the children because I always make sure I am out of town during my custody time and give them to whatever woman I have bamboozled. This time, I made sure I got a really gullible one, I even married her so now I am better than you. I will use "we" now, and never use "I".

I don't know the first thing about my kids, so I have no clue why Kenny is always sick when he is with me, but never sick when he is with you. I am going to pretend this is your fault. It must be your fault, because "we" are perfect. We took him to the ER to be dramatic. I don't like that the children get to have a new house with you, so we are going to ruin it for everyone. We will cause them so much stress that they get sick. We will ignore the pediatrician's directions to bring Kenny back into the office, because we know you have talked to the doctor. We don't like that the pediatrician suspects stress as root cause. We will also bring up something random, off-the-wall and untrue about Noelia to make you look bad. We are just jealous that the kids have fun when they are with you.

You make me so angry that the children are happy and healthy! How dare you! You were supposed to live in a van down by the river! You wicked witch! We also don't care about the court order…like ever…so now I'm not going to send you important medical information (probably because we can't find a doctor to say he is really sick physically and the plan is falling apart so ABORT MISSION). I'm also super jealous that your awesome job provides incredible benefits and you have access to all medical records, and I had to take you to court so you would send me EOB's (even though I don't ever open or read them because I don't understand them..lol..heehee). We will also bully the children into submission by showing them emails between parents, because when all else fails, threaten and bully. I also realize that you are intelligent so I had the new wife write part of this, I cannot formulate a sentence and I wanted to make sure you understood how important and "winning" I am. Winning! At the end of the day, I'm jealous of the world you live in. I will never see it. So I will act like an asshole at every moment I can because I just have no self-control, and I don't need any because I am so friggin special! I'm not really going to file anything because I'd probably loose custody and I can't lose because I'm WINNING! I hate 50/50, and I hope you make it unbearable so I can blame you when my new princess catches on fully to my "secret" and starts getting feisty. I gotta dump the kids then, so be prepared. I think it's starting to happen….I'm going to make you seem like the one who is controlling when it's really me…so when I just give up the struggle and custody, I will get so much sympathy and maybe the princess won't leave me then…. Hatefully, Billy

Suggested Response:

Billy- I will continue to keep you informed of doctor's visits and medical updates. -Susan

The men and women on the battlefield of the Family Court System have secured a place in my heart forever. One of our brave warrior mom's submitted a summary of what it's like in "Narcissistic Bizarro World" and I think she did a fantastic job of capturing a world that so many of us have been forced into.

> My ex-husband lives in "Bizarro World." Let me tell you what lives there. This world consists of their truth, their lies, and their memories of YOUR life. They do not have memories of all the wrongs they did or of the lies they told...only their delusional spin on your life. It's a world created by them to make themselves feel better and to make themselves look better to the real world. My ex-husband can remember conversations we had in 1988 word for word. He can remember where and what I ate while having the conversation that he is recounting. He can remember that I applied two dashes of salt to my mashed potatoes so of course, his recollection must be true. Of course what he remembers is me wanting to leave him for another man. Wow...I sure wish I remembered that! I'm both amazed and entertained by his stories. Sometimes I want to go to Bizarro World so I can change my memories too. I would change the memories of him making me feel bad for being successful, for being a good mom and for loving my family. I would change the memories of my world revolving around him. I would change the memories of always making excuses for his rude and mean behavior towards my family, friends or my children. I would change the memories of allowing him to treat my oldest son like hired help. I would change the memory of how worthless he

made me feel on a daily basis. While I no longer live in his Bizarro World, he continuously invites me to move there and take up residence. Through his warped recollection of my life, I have visited Bizarro World and it's a cold, twisted and lonely place. I prefer the warmth, love and TRUTH I have and cherish in the REAL world. -Anonymous

Seth often emailed me straight from the deep, dark depths of Bizarro World. Here is an example of one such email and how he can cunningly twist reality to suit his agenda. In this particular case, his agenda was to showcase me as unbalanced. Portions of this dialog were included in his court declarations in an effort to make the Judge believe that I was unstable.

> *Tina- Now that I have reviewed your blog, it shows you are suffering from severe mental issues and you need therapy. You showed up at a Broadway Show and asked Christie Brinkley to autograph your divorce papers, then you "burst into tears." This is absolutely telltale of your lack of emotional stability. Tina you are inflicting a split household on our children because that is how you grew up, with feelings of abandonment from your mother, raised by just your father. Your mother suffered from "bipolar personality disorder" which is a genetically transferable condition and you may have this diagnosis as well. -Seth*

Bizarro World: While I empathize with the woman who *did* cry over her divorce papers, it wasn't me. It does however, demonstrate exactly how he twists reality to suit the world that he has created in his head. This is the actual quote from Christie Brinkley that Seth is referencing:

"It was an absolute honor for me to meet Tina Swithin. Every day she is helping women get through a painful period of their life. Last night after my Broadway show, I was greeted at the stage door by a woman who gave me her divorce papers to autograph. I asked her if she was ok and a flood of tears ensued. I understood. I told her to look up, "One Mom's Battle" and that she would find great advice to help her get through divorcing a narcissist. Thank you, Tina for creating a wonderful resource to share!!!! - Christie Brinkley

If you are offered an all-expense paid trip to Bizarro World, refuse the invitation and stay firmly planted in your truth. Bizarro World is built on a foundation of gas lighting, lies, projection and distortion. Even a short scenic drive through the land of Bizarro World is enough to make the strongest people doubt their own sanity. In the infamous Hotel California, guests can "check-out anytime but they can never leave." This is how I picture Bizarro World and the narcissist. They can truly never leave but *you* can. Grab your suitcase, do an about-face and refuse to enter this dark, evil land. You have that choice while the narcissist is destined to be there forever. You are free to check out anytime you like and you *can* actually leave.

CHAPTER 7

FINAL THOUGHTS

When trying to formulate my thoughts on how to end this book, I found myself struggling a bit. First, I hate goodbyes and tend to get a little bit sappy. Writing my first book, "Divorcing a Narcissist: One Mom's Battle" was an emotionally, cathartic journey where I was able to completely purge myself of memories from the most difficult few years of my life. To date, I've never read my own book. While that may sound bizarre to many, I have no desire to relive that portion of my life. I lived the experiences, I wrote about the trials and tribulations that I faced in a very broken system and I then set them loose into the universe where they fused together with stories from all over the world. I've always said that my story is really not *my* story – it's *your* story and the story of thousands of others who have walked this path. I just so happened to *write* it, but my story belongs to anyone who has been victimized by someone with a Cluster B personality disorder.

The Narc Decoder is a book that has been on my heart for several years. I knew it had to be written for several reasons but I also knew that it would involve digging deep into a painful period of my life that I was more than happy to watch fade away in my rearview mirror. When I rolled up my sleeves and began to sort through the mountains of emails and text messages, there were several times that I had to close my computer and walk away from the project. Sometimes I took a

145

break for a few days and other times, I needed a few weeks to regroup. There were some emails that I read with wide eyes, muttering under by breath, "he's bat-shit crazy!" So much of my life during the beginning stages of my custody battle is a blur and so much of it defied logic. I am thankful that I journaled at each step of the journey because that journal morphed into a blog and eventually, a series of books.

If you are reading this book, it probably means that you are experiencing a living hell at the hands of a personality disordered individual. If that descriptions describes you, please consider yourself hugged tightly. When I began my consulting business in 2015, it was my way to get into the trenches with those who are suffering. I quickly realized that this problem was so much bigger than me. I would go to sleep some nights riddled with guilt because I was finding myself unable to answer all of the desperate emails and messages that come through on a daily basis. Writing books is my way of helping those who I haven't had the privilege of meeting, helping or reassuring. Regardless of if we have or haven't met, I am cheering you on from afar. I am holding your hand in spirit. I am praying for you and your children nightly. Any healthy parent who is going to bat for their children is a hero in my book.

My story is your story and your story is the story of someone else halfway around the world. We are united in a sorority or fraternity that you'd never willingly sign up for but once you've been initiated, you are surrounded by some of the most amazing individuals you'll ever meet. While you may feel alone right now, you aren't. Feeling alone is a gut wrenching, soul crushing place to be and I know it well, because I spent quite a bit of time there. On a monthly basis, I speak to women and men from all walks of life – from celebrities to Sunday School teachers and from stay-at-home moms to psychologists. No one is immune to the narcissist's web. They lure their victims forth with their manipulative ways and string us along until we are in a fog so thick that we can't find our way out. Once we are free from their clutches, our survival is dependent on education, therapy and connecting with those who are also on the path to healing. I encourage you to reach out to One Mom's Battle (www.onemomsbattle.com), The Lemonade Club (www.thelemonadeclub.com) or your local women's shelter, domestic violence center, church or a therapist for support. There are so many of us and there is no reason to suffer alone.

Aside from educating yourself on Cluster B personality disorders and connecting with others, it is critical to compartmentalize the pandemonium from this battle. Do not allow this battle to consume your life and rob you of joy. The narcissist wants nothing more than to rob you of joy. It is imperative that you soak in the peaceful times even if that is at the crack of dawn when you are enjoying coffee in your pajamas. The moments of peace will restore you and leave you better equipped to handle the madness. Understanding the language of the narcissist is critical but finding humor wherever you can is life changing. The tools contained in this book helped me to make it to the other side and I hope you find some of them helpful in your own personal journey.

ENDNOTES

Chapter 3
1. 180 Rule, The Gray Rock Method of Dealing with
    Psychopaths, 2012

Chapter 7
1. Swithin, *One Mom's Battle*, 2011

ABOUT THE AUTHOR

Tina Swithin survived a Category Five Life Storm and took shelter by writing her first book in 2012 titled, *"Divorcing a Narcissist: One Mom's Battle."* In 2014, Tina wrote her second book, *"Divorcing a Narcissist: Advice from the Battlefield"* and her third book, *"Divorcing a Narcissist: Rebuilding After the Storm"* followed shortly after.

Tina has dedicated her life to Family Court advocacy and helping those involved in high-conflict custody battles. Tina's internationally recognized blog, *"One Mom's Battle"* was turned into a 501(c)3 non-profit organization in 2015 and she currently serves on the Board of Directors. In addition, Tina has created a private, membership-based forum, *"The Lemonade Club,"* for those fighting to protect their children from personality disordered individuals. Each year, Tina holds a retreat called *"The Lemonade Power Retreat"* for those rebuilding their lives in the aftermath of a high-conflict divorce.

Tina has become a voice for change in the Family Court System after seeing the flaws first-hand. Tina believes that the courts have lost sight of their primary focus, which should be the best interest of the child and instead, are focusing too heavily on parental rights. Tina is working to raise awareness of the issues in the Family Court System and to educate the general public on Cluster B personality disorders. High conflict divorces are on the rise and the children are suffering unnecessarily due to the lack of education on the front lines—and behind the judicial bench.

In the past, Tina has been awarded honors such as the "Top 20 Professionals Under 40" and the "Top 40 Professionals Under 40" in several regional California newspapers. Tina has appeared on shows such as *"Dr. Carole's Couch"* and on Huff Post LIVE. Tina's work has been featured in outlets such as Glamour Magazine, SF Gate, Examiner, LA Parent Magazine, About.com, Yahoo, Huffington Post and the Washington Times. All of Tina's books have garnered 5-star ratings with hundreds of reviews on Amazon. In her spare time, Tina writes for the Huffington Post Divorce where she delves into the tricky world of divorcing a narcissist.

Tina resides in San Luis Obispo, California with her husband, two daughters and Standard Poodle, Pixie.

Made in United States
North Haven, CT
16 August 2022